An Honorable Estate

An Honorable Estate

My Time in
the Working
Press

Louis D. Rubin, Jr.

LOUISIANA STATE ✴ UNIVERSITY PRESS

Baton Rouge

Designer: Amanda McDonald Scallan

Typeface: Bembo

Printer and binder: Thomson-Shore, Inc.

Library of Congress Cataloging-in-Publication Data:

Rubin, Louis Decimus, 1923–

   An honorable estate : my time in the working press / Louis D. Rubin, Jr.

     p. cm.

   ISBN 0-8071-2732-9

   1. Rubin, Louis Decimus, 1923– 2. Journalists—United States—Biography. I. Title.

   PN4874.R75 A3 2001

   070'.92—dc21

2001001765

The paper in this book meets the guidelines for permanence and durability of the
Committee on Production Guidelines for Book Longevity of the Council on Library
Resources. ∞

for Cindy and John MacKethan

Contents

Headnote

The sketches that follow are of a time, back before I gave up working for a living and became a college professor, when my goal in life was to be a newspaperman. In writing them I have had two objectives. I wanted to describe what the practice of daily journalism was like before the advent of television killed off all the afternoon newspapers and ended the reign of morning newspapers as the principal medium for purveying breaking news. And I wanted to try to explain to myself how and why it was that I ended up not pursuing a vocation that from childhood on I had set my sights on following.

In what follows I do not mean for a moment to suggest that there was any failure on the part of the intended vocation; the shortcoming was mine, not journalism's. At the same time, I make no apology for the vocation that I chose in its stead. Certainly I do not regret my decision to become a teacher, though perhaps some of my students do. On the contrary, in the way that things worked out I think I was extraordinarily fortunate.

These sketches do not constitute an autobiography. Some of the most urgent concerns of my life are not addressed in them. Rather, they are, or are meant to be, an account, informal and subjective, of a career that I intended for myself, and of its final forsaking, with just enough about other matters to set the decision in context. I hope that those who read that account will find at least some of it amusing, for it strikes me in retrospect, all things considered, as having been mainly a comedy.

For help in writing and revising this book I am grateful to Guy Friddell, William D. Chamberlain, Paul Duke, Charles McDowell, and Hal Crowther, five first-rate newsmen who, unlike myself, stayed the course; and to two first-rate magazine editors, Staige Blackford and George Core. The sketches entitled "Introduction: An Honorable Profession," "A Term as City Editor," and "Remembrance of Copy Desks Past" were first published, in somewhat different form, in the *Sewanee Review,* and for permission to reprint them I am grateful to the editor, George Core.

Chapel Hill, North Carolina
August 27, 2000

An Honorable Estate

1

INTRODUCTION
An Honorable Profession

In the late 1970s I wrote a novel in which the protagonist, a fifteen-year-old living in a small city in South Carolina, aspired to be a newspaperman. It was autobiographical, not so much in what happened as in the characterization, and was meant to be a kind of portrait of a would-be artist as a teenager. Among the very few reviews that the novel received was one in the *Times Literary Supplement* of London, in which a young Briton named Mars-Hill or Mars-Jones or the like tore into it. The English hierarchical system apparently being still alive and well despite the Empire's diminished grandeur, it was the ambition to be a journalist that seemed most to trigger his ire. The fact that a youth growing up in a middle-class family in the United States in the early decades of the twentieth century might think of a newspaper career in the terms that I had done, which was precisely my point, was totally unacceptable to him. Journalism, for God's sake! he expostulated.

As the late Quentin Compson, who harbored no newspaper intentions, remarked to a Canadian friend on another topic, in order to understand you would have to have been born there; and to be fair to Mr. Mars-Hill, I've no doubt that not merely what he considered to be the lowly nature of my protagonist's vocational aspirations but the way in which these were set forth by the author were what upset him. All the same, if my handling of the matter was unconvincing he might have considered the instances of such as Sherwood Anderson, Theodore Dreiser, W. D. Howells, Ring Lardner, Ernest Hemingway, and H. L. Mencken—assuming that he had heard of them—before dismissing as preposterous the assumption that I was making. For if considered suspect at Oxbridge, in the provinces of the New World the prospect of a future career in journalism could indeed stir emotions that in another place and time would have been appropriate to a vocation as poet.

The newsroom and the print shop were able to lure

some few of us while young by means of a certain near-aphrodisiac that was every bit as potent and evocative as the taste of scalloped wafers steeped in lime-flower tea. It was the aroma of printer's ink, tangy and sour-sweet and tinctured with the somewhat acrid odor of newsprint, and it functioned for our kind as a kind of musk. It could entice otherwise-respectable youths to become enamored of careers in the reporting and writing of the news.

The bouquet of printer's ink, once breathed in under such auspices, was thereafter unmistakable. Mark Sullivan, who inhaled it at the shops of eastern Pennsylvania weekly newspapers in the late 1880s, was walking in Antwerp, Belgium, some years later, when he "felt suddenly a sense at once of pleasure and homesickness, of alertness and longing. Stopping, I realized that it came from something in the air." He traced it to a tiny alley, walked along a dark passageway to a courtyard. "As I entered the court," he wrote in *The Education of an American,* "I felt like a traveler who in a strange land comes miraculously upon blood kin. Before me, in an ancient building, with the smell of printer's ink suffusing the air, was the oldest printing establishment in the world, now taken over by the Belgian government for preservation, the Plantin Museum."

Youths who picked up the scent commonly first did so in job shops where school newspapers were printed or in daily or weekly newspaper plants— wherever printers used breyer rollers to ink forms, pulled proofs on proofpresses, locked up chases, made ready, and printed news in columns of type, whether upon flatbed, cylinder, tubular, or high-speed rotary presses. Ever afterward, and no matter how far removed the careers they later followed, they tended to associate the aroma with the excitement and anticipation that went along with being youthful, ambitious, and journalistically inclined.

All this was back when newspapers were still the preponderant medium of public information, which is to say, from the later nineteenth until the mid–twentieth century. Newspapers continue to be read and are important, of course, and aspiring young people still seek jobs on their staffs. But there are notably fewer daily newspapers extant—in all but a few cities the afternoon newspaper is a thing of the past—and for various and complex reasons, to be a reporter for a newspaper may no longer serve the function that it did for many young men of an earlier epoch: literary *entrée,* the chance to commence a vocation in *writing.*

I do not mean by this that newspapers today are less well-written than they once were; on the contrary, they are probably better written. Nor do I wish to imply that there is less idealism involved in the impulse toward a career in daily journalism. I daresay that today's aspiring newspaperman probably enters the profession with, if anything, even more active zeal and motivation for exposing the injustices and crimes and righting the wrongs of society than was true for earlier generations. What is known as investigative reporting, whereby such objectives are energetically pursued, is far more common and useful today than ever it used to be.

Still, I have the sense that the ambition to secure a position in journalism at the present time does not typically involve what was once so often bound in with the desire to be a reporter: the impulse, however yet unfocused and undifferentiated, toward literary assertion. Perhaps this is because secondary schools, colleges, and universities regularly offer courses and programs in creative writing, as back in the Dark Ages they decidedly did not. Thus the impulse to write as a means of expressing one's personal emotions may nowadays be differentiated from other modes of writing at a more larval stage of development than formerly. Knowing better what he or she is seeking, today's ambitious would-be poet or novelist or dramatist may set out with a clearer vocational path specifically in mind.

But at the time I am writing about, for a young

man who was reasonably bright, curious about what went on around him, and who felt the urge to express himself* in writing, employment as a newspaper reporter was alluring because it offered, or appeared to offer, an opportunity to write. Whether in news stories, features, editorials, or bylined columns, a newspaperman could earn a living through the act of using written language descriptively, which was more than could be said of other available forms of employment.

Although a daily newspaper was privately owned and was designed to be profit-making, those on its news staff did not think of it on those terms, or see their duties as those of hired hands in a business venture. Rather, they viewed themselves as, for want of a better word, craftsmen—which is to say, as professional men engaged in an activity the objective of which was altruistic or, more accurately, noncommercial. Perhaps a vocation in a priesthood would be an even better

* I may as well say that in writing of those who were future journalists in the days of my apprenticeship I will be using the masculine gender throughout, because back then, on most newspapers of any size the chances of a young woman's being taken on as a reporter were decidedly poor. The only opportunity that commonly arose for a young woman with an ambition to be a journalist was with the society page—or women's page, as it was beginning to be called on papers that were notably progressive-minded—where engagements, weddings, social occasions, recipes, and fashions were recorded.

metaphor, exacting vows of poverty if not of obedience and chastity. A calling to write the news, to put into print what was important or interesting or amusing about a community's life, was held to be an activity fully as valuable, and as consecrated and nonpartisan, as that of healing the sick, teaching the young, enforcing the law and meting out justice, caring for the poor, ministering to the sinful, or creating works of art.

The upper echelons of the newspaper organization—the publisher, the editors, the advertising executives—might have their axes to grind, and might have their reasons to wish the news interpreted in order to achieve certain objectives and turn a profit. The reporter, for his part, observed and reported objectively on what he saw. However humble his particular assignment or lowly his status, he wrote up the news as he found it, and unless on the sports staff would ordinarily think twice before allowing a politico or a financial tycoon to buy him a dope, as Coca-Colas were still called back in those quaint days. (In sports the ethics of the profession were less restrictive, though outright payola was taboo.)

Yet if the young newsman thought of himself as following a profession, rather than merely holding down a job, it was one that differed from most other professions, in that he was not an independent contractor but a salaried employee. The pay for an apprentice newspaperman ranged from poor to abominable. For the privilege of writing for a living instead of selling, clerking, or otherwise holding down a white-collar job, a bright young man learned to get by on what even for the times were minuscule wages, with no more than modest increases thereafter. Starting out on the *Baltimore Herald* in 1898, H. L. Mencken was paid $7 a week. Will Irwin, beginning on the *San Francisco Chronicle* in 1900, might earn as much as $20 a week on space rates if he was lucky and received numerous assignments, but there was no guarantee of it, and more often he took home scarcely half that.

Theodore Dreiser's starting salary on the *Chicago Globe* in the early 1890s, after he had worked for a few dollars a week at space rates for more than a month, was $15, the same as Ernest Hemingway's on the *Kansas City Star* in 1916, a quarter-century later. Twenty years after that, in 1936, when Vermont Royster went to work for the *Wall Street Journal* in New York City, he too received $15 a week.

Those were big-city papers. When in the late 1900s an uncle of mine worked for three months on the staff of the *News and Courier,* in Charleston, South Carolina, it was without any salary at all. The arrangement was that he and another young man would both try out for a vacant post on the staff, which would pay $7 a week, and at the end of that time one of them would be given it. My uncle, who later became a playwright, had only a seventh-grade education. His rival was a college graduate, and the disparity in background was too much to overcome; the other youth got the job.

As things turned out, his quest proved not to be in vain, for he had acquitted himself well, and when word came over the Associated Press telegraph wire that there was a beginning reporter's spot open on a paper in Birmingham, he was recommended for it and got that job.

Why was my uncle willing to enter into such an arrangement, for a job that paid so little? (Surely he must have received some recompense during the period of trying out, in the way of space rates or the like, for the family was extremely poor and he could not have otherwise afforded it.) The motivation is obvious: because he wanted to *write* for a living. With only a seventh-grade education—like his three brothers, another of whom also became a newspaperman, he had to go to work once he completed elementary school—but impelled by the desire to write, he found newspaper reporting the sole option open to him. To write for a newspaper was a move in the direction of a career in letters. It was a way to work with words.

I do not mean by this that a youthful journalist

customarily saw himself as forced to write news stories because he could not earn a living writing fiction or poetry. The point is that in his mind the two modes were still largely undifferentiated. To an extent that may no longer be true, they were part and parcel of the same impulse.

To understand what newspaper work was, it is important to keep that in mind. Particularly in late nineteenth century and in the earlier decades of the twentieth, it simply did not occur to most youths from families without college backgrounds or ties to the learned professions to make any hard-and-fast distinction between journalism and literature. To secure a reporter's job could be the opening step of a literary career. If someone wanted to write, and wasn't independently wealthy, as a matter of course he sought a reporter's job.

The national letters reflect this. From the post–Civil War period onward into the era of Ernest Hemingway, an apprenticeship at writing the news often provided a doorway to the writing of fiction. Not coincidentally, the American novel was realistic or naturalistic in its aesthetic. Our literature was learning to include in its purview a far wider slice of everyday experience, particularly urban experience, than had previously been true.

To incorporate this new subject matter for literary

purposes, what was needed was an access to middle-class and working-class life in terms of its own values, rather than those of an older, more elevated and leisured cultural situation. A necessary part of the writer's equipment was the ability to see and identify what was actually in place around him; documenta-tion—journalism—became an important artistic tool. It has been said of William Dean Howells, who pio-neered in American realism, that for him the absence of culture could still be viewed only as a deprivation; whereas for Theodore Dreiser, who began on daily newspapers in Chicago and St. Louis, it was seen as a fact.

The newspapermen I have in mind were those who first went in search of reportorial work during roughly a 75-year-period, between about 1875 and 1950, or shortly after World War II ended. They tended to come from middle-class families and were generally short on inherited or endowed funds. The desire for wealth and affluence, however, was insufficiently com-pelling, and thus did not immediately steer them in the direction of business and industry, where making money was an acknowledged and primary motivation. Instead, what they wanted most was to see what they wrote appear in print.

It would not be accurate to say that a majority of

them wished to become authors of books, although not a few did so become. More often the act of writing, the pleasure of arranging thoughts and images in words for the sake of self-expression as such, was not their sole motivating goal. They also desired to be involved in what was happening in the life going on around them, and to participate in it through reporting.

Being a newspaperman offered a role, a vantage point. One could play a part in what was happening, be privy to its strivings and its secrets, without being morally or financially committed to its various undertakings and enlisted as a partisan in the struggle itself. The newsman was not doer, but observer and chronicler. He did not engage directly in politics, law enforcement, civic, commercial, cultural, and social ventures. Yet his role in public affairs was acknowledged and respected. What he would write about a given event was important, and those who were involved knew it, coveted it, and even sometimes feared it.

Some newspapermen were college-educated, others weren't, although as time went on a college education, if not quite a prerequisite, became more and more advantageous to what they aspired to do. Still, what was more important than having been formally and substantially exposed to a body of academic knowledge was the ability to describe and interpret what people in government, business, society, educa-

tion, sports—the daily activities of a community—
were engaged in doing.

No insignificant number of journalists, whatever their
reasons for wanting to become newspaper reporters,
eventually found the writing of straight news either
boring over the long run, or else insufficiently remu-
nerative, or both. For such persons, the only way to
stay permanently in daily journalism *as* a writer of
news while also getting into the upper echelons in re-
spect to salary and prestige was to become a specialist
and/or columnist. What was ironic about being a
newspaperman was that in most instances the reward
for excellence in writing the news was elevation to a
position in which one no longer wrote it, but edited
what others wrote. To remain a journalist while also
prospering financially therefore meant either the desk
or else, if exceptionally skilled, a move to the Big
Time.

So the newsman who advanced in his profession
usually became a city editor or managing editor, or
else moved to a larger newspaper, where if he continued to advance he eventually did the same. Otherwise,
if he had a pronounced flair for writing, he might become a columnist. Or he might leave daily newspapering to write articles for magazines. Some few went
on to become novelists, playwrights, even poets. Many

more, often through the associations they developed as journalists, became publicists, corporate and business executives, public officials. Or they went into other forms of journalism, or into book publishing, or the entertainment industry. Or they returned to universities for graduate study and became academics. Or whatever.

Newspaper salaries did not really begin to improve significantly until the 1950s. In the years just after World War II, the going wage was up to $30 or $35, which in terms of the cost of living was no better than Ernest Hemingway's $15 in 1916. My pay as a reporter in northern New Jersey in 1946 was $33. But with the widening of economic opportunities, daily newspapers were by then finding it increasingly difficult to hold onto their more experienced reporters. The American Newspaper Guild also played a role in getting reportorial salaries increased. The typographical and mechanical employees on newspapers had long been organized; their craft unions had evolved directly out of the old-time guilds. Not so the reporters. Needless to say, management was not averse to taking full advantage of the fact, with the result that a linotype operator or a pressman working in a city with a typographical union chapel, as they were called, customarily received double and even triple the weekly recompense of a reporter of comparable experience.

There were numerous reasons why unionization

came late to newsrooms. For one thing, unlike typesetting and printing, there was no particular techno-
logical skill involved in covering the news; one learned
as one went along, and manual and physical dexterity
at setting type and handling machinery was not required. The ways of the writer and the typesetter
began diverging in the mid–nineteenth century, when
newspapers became larger and more specialized. The
advent of high-speed printing presses, electroplating
and stereotyping, and, later in the century, mechanical
typesetting brought an end to the days when young
men such as Samuel L. Clemens, William Dean Howells, and Joel Chandler Harris began their careers as
jour printers, learning to set type by hand, and then
took to composing editorial squibs on their own. Except perhaps on small-town weeklies, by the turn of
the century the separation of newsroom and composing room was almost total.

At least as important was the manner in which the
reporter viewed himself and what he was doing. It was
not merely that he did not think of himself as a la-
borer, a purveyor of manual skills such as a printer, or a
plumber, or a railroad engineer. It was also that he
considered himself no trained workman but the prac-
titioner of a profession. However humble his position
on a news staff, he cherished his independence, his sin-
gularity. The idea that he was no more than a hired
journeyman, paid to work a stated number of hours

per week in order to produce a commodity designed to be sold at a profit to the owner, was an affront to his self-esteem, to the image he bore of himself as journalist and gentleman. The result was that generations passed before most newspaper reporters could expect to receive salaries that were roughly comparable to those of their contemporaries in other fields of work.

Daily journalism was not, in its early days, a notably respectable occupation. The image of the old-time newspaperman was of one who drank and gambled, frequently quit or was fired, moved from paper to paper, and was generally improvident and unreliable. Eugene Field, who worked on the *Denver Tribune* and elsewhere as reporter and editor before settling down in Chicago as a columnist for the *Daily News,* wrote and illustrated a funny little book, *The Tribune Primer,* first published in Denver in 1882. It contained a number of comic depictions of the newspaperman of the mid-nineteenth-century era, including the following:

THE BOTTLE

This is a Bottle. What is in the Bottle? Very bad Whiskey. It has been Sent to the Local Editor. He did not Buy it. If he had Bought it the Whiskey would have been Poorer than it is. Little Children, you Must never Drink Bad Whiskey.

THE CITY EDITOR

Here we Have a City Editor. He is Talking with the Foreman. He is saying he will have a Full Paper in the Morning. The Foreman is Smiling Sadly. Maybe he is Thinking the Paper will have a Full City Editor before Morning.

By the 1880s, however, the circumstances of daily newspaper publishing were undergoing striking changes in the direction of far greater comprehensiveness, reliability, efficiency, and professional respectability. Newspapers became larger, made greater distinction between news and opinion, and grew both in circulation and in community position and function. They ceased to exist primarily as organs for political parties and factions, and became business ventures. The roles of editor and publisher diverged. Where once capital enough to rent one floor of a small building, purchase a flatbed press and an assortment of type, hire a jour printer to set it, ink the chases, and pull off impressions, and a newsboy or two to deliver copies to subscribers and hawk them on the main street was all that was needed for a young man to set himself up in the newspaper business, the daily newspaper now required a considerable investment in equipment and personnel. Newspapers were now aimed at family as

well as adult male readership. They became dependent
upon advertising rather than the sale of copies for operating revenue; newspapers battled for larger circulation in order to be able to increase rates for advertising
space.

As newspapers gained in scope and respectability,
and accurate, objective reporting became separated
from partisan editorial coloration of the news, there
was no longer a place in newsrooms for the old-style
roistering journeyman paragrapher. Young men now
entered newspaper work as a profession; they wanted
to learn how to write the news and to advance themselves, whether to positions of larger responsibility and
pay on local news staffs or to jobs on larger, more prestigious newspapers.

Although the demand for newspaper reporters increased vastly—there were 850 daily newspapers in the
United States in 1880; twenty years later there were
1,967, and the size of reportorial staffs was expanding
by at least the same proportion—at no point was there
ever a shortage of young men (and, here and there,
young women) eager to fill that demand. For many
such would-be journalists a reporter's position was the
means of upward mobility. My own family is an example; for both of my uncles, attending high school,
much less college, was beyond their economic reach.
A reporter's job meant for them an opportunity to

move solidly into a status that was far closer to that of professional men than would otherwise have been possible without a college education.

Yet, as noted earlier, that was only part of it. They wanted to be newspapermen because they wanted to write, because they thought it would be exciting, glamorous, prestigious. Their attitude toward life and their place in it, however they might learn to mask it under a cloak of cynicism, was essentially romantic; the world was a place of endless variety and opportunity, an ocean of possibilities, and a job as a reporter on a newspaper was a river opening onto that ocean.

There was a naïveté about the way that such things were viewed back then. I think of a passage in Theodore Dreiser's *Newspaper Days* (1922), the second volume of *A Book about Myself,* in which Dreiser tells of being sent out, as a reporter on the *St. Louis Globe-Democrat,* to interview renowned visitors to the city:

> And there were distinguished individuals, including such excellent lecturers as Henry Watterson and Henry M. Stanley, or a musician like Paderewski, or a scientist of the standing of Nikola Tesla. I was sent to interview my share of these, to get their views on something— anything or nothing, really, for my city editor, Mr. Mitchell, seemed at times a little cloudy as to their significance, and certainly I had no clear

insight into what most of them stood for. I
wondered, guessed, made vague stabs at what I
thought they represented, and in the main took
them seriously enough. My favorite question
was what did they think of life, its meaning,
since this was uppermost in my mind at the
time, and I think I asked it of every one of
them, from John L. Sullivan to Annie Besant.

Dreiser was the consummate romantic, the epitome
of the dreaming, ambitious youth who saw the
newspaper city room as the avenue to fame and fortune. Of immigrant stock, reared in abysmal poverty in
the Midwest and knowing actual want, awkward, un-
cultured, hungry for status, wealth, sex, recognition, he
hung around the newsroom of a second-rate Chicago
daily for weeks until finally given an assignment during a political convention. From Chicago he went to
St. Louis, then to Toledo, Cleveland, Pittsburgh, and ultimately to New York City, where he found himself
unable to compete successfully in daily journalism and
took to magazine writing, at which he did very well.

In its intensity, its exaggeration, and its earnestness,
Newspaper Days is the classic presentation, moving and
revelatory, of what made ambitious young Americans
of the early twentieth century covet positions on
newspaper staffs, and what they thought of themselves

as doing when they entered journalism. Except for *Sister Carrie* I like it best of all his books, perhaps because, in the illumination that Dreiser's literary skill could give an experience common to so many who were without his genius, I recognize aspects of my own youthful self in it.

I think, too, of my own newspaperman uncles, in particular the older of the two, Dan. The circumstances of their childhood was not so squalid as Dreiser's. They too were poor, and there was a period of several years in the early 1900s when both their parents were ill and together with my father they were sent to live at the Hebrew Orphan Home in Atlanta, but there was far more culture, kindness, and gentility in their family and their situation. Dan worked as a stock boy at a paper company upon completing the seventh grade, and read voraciously. After he got the job on the staff of the newspaper in Birmingham, he never returned to Charleston to live. From all I have been able to gather he became an excellent newspaperman. I once applied for a job on a newspaper, and the managing editor, noting that I had grown up in Charleston, asked me whether I was any kin to a Dan Rubin, with whom he had worked in Birmingham a quarter-century or more earlier. Anyone related to Dan Rubin, he told me, was likely to be worth his weight in gold in a city room.

Dan stayed in Birmingham until the early 1920s, with time out for service as an infantry lieutenant in France, where he was severely wounded during the Argonne fighting, then worked as reporter and city editor on newspapers in Fort Worth, Texas, Jacksonville, Florida, and Columbia, South Carolina. Early on, his literary interests focused on drama. He began writing plays, and after several were produced on Broadway he left newspaper work and concentrated on that. From the mid-1920s to the early 1930s he had six Broadway productions, two of which were made into movies. In the early 1930s he was offered and accepted a well-paying position writing movie scripts for Paramount Studios in Hollywood, which he did for a half-dozen years. Thereafter he returned to playwriting, which he did for the rest of his life, but never had another accepted for production. I asked him once why he had left newspaper work, and he told me that eventually he found it boring.

My other newspaper uncle, Manning, a year younger than Dan, got a job on the staff of the *Charleston Evening Post* in 1914, when he was twenty-one years old, and stayed there until he retired in the early 1960s. In the mid-1930s he became city editor, then from the early 1940s onward wrote editorials and a daily column. As a young man he wrote fiction, publishing short stories in the popular adventure magazines of the 1910s, but thereafter gave it up.

He spent his time reading (he especially liked books on archaeology and classical history), listening to classical music on his phonograph, and bicycling around downtown Charleston, where a corps of small children waited for his daily afternoon visits. He was one of the most beloved citizens of his city; when he died in 1967 there was a throng in attendance at his funeral, and both local newspapers carried editorials about him.

Would either of my uncles have lived the lives that they did without the opportunity that newspaper work presented them as young men? It is impossible to say, of course. But it seems obvious to me that for many young Americans, to be a reporter on a daily newspaper was the equivalent, during the years between the Civil War and World War I, of what a college education was in later decades—not merely a job, but a means of education.

Recently I happened upon a book entitled *Media Rare: Adventures of a Grass-Roots Newsman,* by Nat Boynton. It is an account, factual and unpretentious, of Mr. Boynton's career as a newspaperman in New York State. He graduated from college and found a job as a reporter on a small daily newspaper. So did I. After a brief period of apprenticeship in the newsroom he was given responsibility for reporting the news from a smaller community within the paper's circulation area. So was I. He was drafted into the Army in World War II, as I was, and served without incident in an area located far distant from the fighting, as did I, the only difference being that Mr. Boynton's time in the military came after several years of reportorial work, while mine preceded my first job on a daily newspaper.

Afterward he moved on to another, smaller daily newspaper, where he worked as a deskman, taking considerable pleasure at page makeup and design. So did I. He was next offered a position in a regional bureau of the Associated Press, as was I, but found his duties there repetitious and boring, whereupon he left daily newspaper work, which is what I did too, and for much the same reasons. Thereafter our paths diverged. Mr. Boynton became a publicist for General Electric, then freelanced, and ultimately bought a small suburban weekly, which he operated successfully until retirement. I did none of those things.

Clearly Mr. Boynton's newspaper experience and mine, up to the point at which we both quit our jobs at the AP, bore marked similarities, although he stayed at each of his various posts longer than I did. Setting out with kindred opportunities, we encountered numerous experiences common to us both. We would have been, I think, congenial colleagues. The differences lay in our attitudes toward what we were doing and why we wanted to do it. It struck me, upon reading his engaging book about a useful and satisfying career as a newspaperman, that from my standpoint it might well have been entitled *The Route Not Taken*.

It is the years when I had set out along that same route that I propose to examine in this book. For almost as far back as I can remember, daily journalism was the vocation I intended for myself. As soon as I was done with the Army and graduated from college I went looking for a newspaper reporter's job, tried journalism in several forms, left it briefly with the intention of returning, stayed out of it longer than I had planned, then tried it once more before I was ready to concede that it was not to be my vocation after all.

The profession of newspapering was certainly not to blame for my failure to stay with it. On the contrary, I believe that all along there was a deficiency within myself that made me unsuited for the job. In the chapters that follow I should like to try to figure out, to my own satisfaction if not necessarily to that of others, what that deficiency was.

"I used to be a newspaperman myself," as they say. The words are customarily spoken with a trace of regret in one's voice, as if claiming a privilege that was once valid but is no longer, yet without apology. That is how I think I feel about it. Having spent a few years in it, followed by more than four decades outside of it, I continue to think of daily journalism as constituting as honest, and as honorable, a profession as exists. In any event the reader, I hope, will be able to judge for himself.

\#　　\#　　\#

2

JOINING THE WORKING PRESS

I was ten years old and lived on Rutledge Avenue just below the Colonial Lake in Charleston, South Carolina, in 1934 when I published my first newspaper. It was called *The Bulliten,* and I typed it in two columns on my father's portable. Among the contents of the issue was a recipe for a bean dish, copied from a Shredded Wheat box, but somewhere in the editorial process the beans got dropped out of the ingredients.

To attain a press run of twelve copies, each page of *The Bulliten* had to be typed three times, an original and three carbons, and even at that the third carbon was so blurred as to be only semilegible. My father, pleased at my enterprise but alarmed at the prospect of his portable being employed as a printing press on a regular basis, bought me a ream of onionskin paper and a very old used Rex standard typewriter. The latter proved so cumbersome that it was soon replaced with a used but less ancient Underwood No. 5. Over the next couple of years *The Bulletin*—the spelling was emended for the second issue—went through a half-dozen or so issues, until at age twelve I entered high school and went out for the school newspaper.

In the summer of 1937, when I was thirteen, I did attempt to publish a newspaper for the city playgrounds, but it never got past the first two-page issue, and cost my father $12 to settle the printing bill. A lifelong precedent was thereby established—the financial flop, that is, not the bail-out by my father. But it was the high school newspaper, the *Bantam,* that mattered. For four years, from September until June, my existence centered on it. In my senior year I was elected editor, and no subsequent development in my life ever so monstrously inflated my self-esteem.

When the school term began, on the first day of classes my Latin teacher, Maurice McLaughlin, called me aside. It was all very well to be editor of the *Bantam,* he told me, but I was not to let it interfere with my preparation for classes—meaning Latin, the previous term of which I had passed only on a reexamination after being tutored over the summer. He counseled in vain; on the first monthly test I scored a

17—the passing mark was 70. I flunked the term outright, switched to a course in Business English, and
graduated in June after another reexam, this one in algebra. Fritz Muller, the algebra teacher, who had already informed my parents that I was not college material, warned me that I would never be able to pass
college mathematics. About the latter he was almost
but not quite correct; the passing mark for freshman
math at the College of Charleston was 65 and I got a
67.

What I was no good at was anything involving
memorizing, for to do so required concentration, an
attribute that was alien to whatever capabilities I possessed at the time. Writing was my principal talent.
During my senior year in high school I had begun
writing for the afternoon newspaper, the *Charleston
Evening Post,* of which my Uncle Manning was city
editor. Mainly I wrote sports; the paper did not have
a full-time sports editor and was happy to have someone covering local athletic events, instead of having to
rewrite the stories in the morning newspaper, the
News and Courier, and the more so because there was
no payment whatever involved. (This, too, was to my
parents' dismay.)

Why did I do it? Certainly I should have liked to
be paid even small sums on space rates; money was not
exactly a plentiful quantity in my life. But the *Evening*

Post had no space rates budget, and it was more important to me to write than to get paid for doing so. (Still another dismaying precedent.) Even so, the pure joy of employing words descriptively was not all that was involved. To see one's byline in bold type atop an account of a football or baseball game was also a distinct source of satisfaction, and to write articles about sports conferred status in athletic circles, which in high school carried weight—more so, alas, than did scholastic or intellectual eminence.

Yet at the bottom of my eagerness to write for the newspaper, for remuneration if possible (it almost never was) but if not to do it anyway, was the basic motivation underlying all writing of other than a purely utilitarian sort: the urge to re-create and so define one's experience in language. As for why newspaper writing as such, the answer is that, in the time and place of my growing up, no other form of writing was being encouraged, and for no other kind of writing was publication a possibility.

At the High School of Charleston there was no literary magazine, and no extracurricular literary society; there was not even a yearbook. None of the teachers of my literature classes ever displayed the slightest interest in any imaginative writing that a student might do. I daresay that at the merest hint of encouragement I would have deluged such a teacher with fiction and poetry—so their indifference may not have been such a bad idea at that. But as it was, if one wanted to be published, read, achieve at least a modicum of recognition, and to be involved *as* a writer in what was going on, writing for newspapers was what one did.

By the time I entered college, there was no doubt in my mind what I would be upon graduation: a newspaper reporter. No other career even so much as suggested itself. It was the one thing that I was good at. As for a possible vocation as a teacher, it never crossed my mind; except in literature and history courses it was all I could do to get passing marks.

My first salaried job for news writing came in the summer following my first year of college, in 1941. I was paid $8 a week to be the reporter, sports editor, and general factotum for a weekly newspaper in the industrial area north of the city, which was burgeoning with defense installations. I held the job for a couple of months. After my sophomore year my family moved to Richmond, Virginia, and during my junior year at the University of Richmond I worked in the news bureau and alumni office writing press releases.

Then came the Army. I was inducted in June 1943 and discharged two years and eight months later, in January 1946. During that time I proved an absolute disaster as an infantry trainee, came close to flunking out of the Army Specialized Training Program in Italian area and language studies at Yale University, showed myself incompetent as a clerk in an ordnance battalion headquarters, and was then put to work writing news stories and editing a newspaper at Fort Benning, Georgia. It was not exactly a distinguished military career; fortunately the American war effort did not depend upon what I could contribute to it. That the Army, despite being busy trying to win a war, not only tolerated me but ultimately even set me to doing something at which I did prove to have competence is, in retrospect, astounding. Thankfully, after an agonizingly slow start I managed to do a reasonable amount of growing up, especially during the last year or so, and also a great deal of reading, so that when I returned to college in February of 1946 for my final year, I was no longer a borderline case as a scholar.

I even thought briefly—very briefly—of going on for graduate study: in history, not in literature. But newspaper work was where my ambition lay. I was certain of that. Even before I began looking around I received telegrams from newspapers in Columbus, Georgia, and Knoxville, Tennessee, offering reporting jobs to me on the strength of recommendations by friends I had known in the Army.

Meanwhile, however, I had gotten myself engaged to a girl who lived in northern New Jersey, and it was there that I wanted to work. The *Bergen Evening Record,* in Hackensack, offered me a reporter's job at a salary of $33 a week, and I accepted at once, for Hackensack was right across the river from Teaneck, where my girlfriend lived. When the summer school term ended in late August I collected my diploma and headed North, aged twenty-two, ready at last to begin the career I had planned for myself since the age of ten.

The *Bergen Record* was published for readers in the numerous small cities, townships, and suburbs of Bergen County, across the Hudson River from New York City, many of whom commuted to and from Manhattan. Each afternoon the *Record* contained a modicum of national and international news, but mainly it operated on the assumption that most of its subscribers read either the *Times, Herald-Tribune,* or *Daily News* in the morning, and that no small number of them picked up an afternoon New York paper en route home after work.

What they could not find in any of those was news about the goings-on in their home communities, and this the *Record* offered in abundance. Its competition was not with the metropolitan dailies, but with the various weeklies throughout the area. These in their turn could furnish even more local material than the *Record* about the individual towns where they were published, but only the *Record* could provide the breaking news in those towns—police, fires, the courts, local government in general.

For its size and circulation, in the forty thousands,

the *Record* employed a large staff of reporters, who concentrated on local news. Seldom did happenings in the assorted small New Jersey communities within its coverage attract much attention other than within Bergen County. Still, when I think back on what I was writing about in those days, it seems to me that, albeit in a minor key, certain problems that I faced as a news reporter were among the basic issues that have confronted journalism in our time. They have by no means been satisfactorily resolved; the advent of television news has only broadened their relevance.

For the first month or so after I arrived in Hackensack I worked in the newsroom as one of several beginning reporters. After I had been on the job for a couple of days the city editor, Jim Sutphen, called me over for a conference. "Well, at least we won't have to teach you how to write," he began. I would be working out of the newsroom for some weeks, he said, after which I would be assigned to a regular beat. In the days that followed I took stories over the telephone, wrote obituaries from information received from funeral homes, and was occasionally sent out to cover automobile wrecks and the like.

About three weeks after I had begun work I was in the newsroom by myself late in the afternoon, writing a story, when the telephone rang. It was one of the other beginning reporters. He was in Rutherford, a town seven miles from Hackensack, and there was a big fire downtown, he said.

All the editors had left for the day, and none of the senior reporters was present. I told him to find out what was happening and call back. Ten minutes later he called to say the fire was in the back of a large downtown furniture store and the street was cordoned off. It was obvious that he had no idea of how to handle the situation. I told him to stay there and find out everything he could, and I would be there shortly. I found a taxicab and went speeding down Route 17 toward Rutherford. The smoke from the fire was visible from some distance.

When I arrived, a block of the main street had been roped off and a sizable crowd was behind the barrier looking on. No flames were visible, but there was a thick smell of burnt wood in the air, and smoke was rising from in back of the building. Fire hose lines led into the two-story building from several fire trucks, which in turn were connected to nearby hydrants. At least a half-dozen fire trucks were on the scene, including several lengthy hook-and-ladder vehicles. Ladders led up onto the roof, where firemen were moving about.

The reporter was standing across the street from the store, waiting for me. He had learned the name of the furniture store and its proprietor and, so far as I could tell, nothing else. I told him to try to find the owner of the store, get an estimate of the value of the contents of the store and the building, and whether it was insured. I would go looking for the fireman in charge.

At the rear of the building was a place where a half-dozen firemen seemed to be grouped, just outside an entrance with double doors. They were wearing helmets and raincoats, and several of them held axes. One of the firemen had a badge on his helmet indicating that he was the chief. When I told him that I was a newspaper reporter, that seemed to be an Open Sesame, for at once he began to tell me all about the fire, when, where, and how it appeared to have first broken out, what kind of equipment was used to fight it, and so on. I asked questions and took notes on everything.

I peered through the double doors. The interior was dark, but I could see flashlights moving about and a dim orange glow in the distance. "Don't go in there without a helmet," the chief told me. "Have you got one?"

"No." It did not occur to me to think I would actually be allowed inside the burning building.

"Better go get one off the truck," he said.

I went over to the nearest fire truck, collected a

wide-brimmed metal helmet from a cluster fastened to the side of the cab, and headed for the open doors, feeling much like the late Richard Harding Davis as he approached San Juan Hill in 1898. Immediately inside the building several firemen were standing around. "How's it going?" I asked.

"It's still smoldering," one of them said, "but we've pretty much got it under control now. Don't go any further than right here." He trained a spotlight to illuminate the high ceiling above us. "We had to put a lot of water up there," he said, "and it might give way."

I asked whether there was likelihood of the fire spreading to adjacent buildings. Not any more, I was told, though at first there had been danger of just that happening, which was why so many fire trucks were on the scene.

After a time I went back outside. The other reporter was standing across the street just inside the roped-off area. He had been unable to find the owner, he said. I asked a nearby policeman, who at once pointed him out to us. The owner estimated his loss to be at least a half-million dollars. He wasn't sure what had caused the fire to break out, he said.

The reporter and I agreed that he would stay at the scene for a while longer and call me if there were further developments, while I returned to the office. So I took a taxicab back and began writing the story.

While I was at work the other reporter's father called, and I told him his son was off covering a fire.

"So he's on the job, is he?" his father asked.

"Yes, sir," I told him. "He certainly is."

There were no further calls from the reporter, so presumably the roof of the building did not fall in. I finished writing the story and left it for the night desk man.

The episode was exciting, particularly wearing the fire helmet and going inside the building. I felt a little awkward about having taken over the story, but if I had not done so there would have been nothing to report other than what could be copied off the fire department records in the morning. The other reporter had shown no initiative in finding out what was going on, and made no effort to talk to the firemen or go inside the building to see for himself. (As it turned out, it was not long before he left the *Record* staff to pursue another line of work, which all things considered would appear to have been a wise move on his part.)

A few days afterward I got to cover a far bigger story. Word came that a bus, bearing residents of New York City bound for Suffern, New York, and the Catskills for the Jewish High Holy Days, had collided head-on with a truck while both vehicles were attempting to pass on a three-lane highway near Paramus, just north of Hackensack. At least seven people were known to have been killed. The staff photographer, Charlie Roth, was being sent to the scene of the wreck, and I was to go to the hospital where the dead and injured were being taken by ambulance.

When I arrived, it was to find numerous people, mostly middle-aged or older and some of them bandaged, sitting around in a lounge outside the emergency room. A police lieutenant gave me the names and addresses of the people who had been killed, one of them the bus driver. Several other persons were in critical condition and might not live, he told me. "Those three-lane highways, they're deathtraps," he declared. "We'll never build any more of them." I talked with a hospital spokesman and with various passengers who had been aboard the bus. Most seemed to be in a state of shock, as if they could scarcely believe what had happened. I got as many names and addresses as I could. Meanwhile people were arriving in search of parents and relatives, and there was much weeping and embracing.

I wrote a story about the wreck and a sidebar describing the scene at the hospital. When the first edition came off the press and copies were brought up to the newsroom, there they were, with a photograph of the smashed vehicles, a headline on the front page in very black type, and the sidebar next to it under a ragged-box headline. I read them over and over again.

The managing editor, Rossman Wynkoop, informed me that I had done a good job, and that "you'll find a little something extra in your pay envelope on Friday."

The "little something" brought the total in my pay envelope to $38 instead of $33. Technically I was still on space rates, and would be until given a regular beat. By now, what with the bus wreck and the fire before that, I was beginning to feel that the newspaper business was everything I had imagined it could be in the way of excitement. There was no telling what I might get to write about next.

It was not long, however, before I found out that there was more to being a newspaper reporter than covering breaking stories of fires and bus wrecks. I was assigned to the Teaneck beat, with a five-dollar raise in pay. This meant that I was now responsible for everything that went on in a city of about 30,000 inhabitants. Teaneck was a "bedroom" community; it had no industries, and a large portion of its adult male citizenry commuted to New York City. Each morning I rode the bus over to the small business district, called at the town manager's office, checked the police blotter, and stopped in at the fire department and the board of education. The town council and the traffic court convened at night on alternate weeks, and I was on hand for those. I alternated attendance at several of the weekly service club luncheon meetings, and wrote feature stories about local topics whenever I could find an appropriate subject.

Covering local politics and government was not the kind of newspaper reporting that I was good at. To do it well meant establishing personal ties with assorted politicos and town government officials, and to gain their confidence it was necessary to do some casual but persistent socializing with office secretaries, clerks, police sergeants, and the like on a daily basis. But socializing was not my skill; I was shy, with no gift for making small talk. The immediate result was that within a few weeks of taking over the beat, I got roundly scooped on local political stories by the weekly *Teaneck Sun*. This made Jim Sutphen less than happy.

Then purely by luck something happened that considerably improved my access to what took place on the Teaneck beat. Late one evening, just as I stopped by police headquarters, a telephone call came in. The sergeant on duty answered, and after a moment he turned to another policeman and told him that someone at an address in north Teaneck had reported that something seemed wrong about the house next door. Then he went racing out to a squad car and drove off. I hurried out to the company car I was using that evening and followed him.

It was a drive of a mile or so. When I got there the sergeant had gone over to a window of the house in question and was aiming a flashlight into it. The night was bitterly cold, and the window glass appeared to have a mottled look. As I watched he sprinted back to his squad car and radioed the Teaneck fire department. Within minutes a fire siren could be heard, and not long afterward a pair of fire trucks came roaring up. The firemen went around to the back of the house, and I watched them don smoke masks and oxygen canisters and, armed with fire extinguishers and flashlights, enter the house by a rear door.

While waiting to see what would happen, I talked with the next-door neighbor who had called the police, and made notes. After a time one of the firemen came outside via the front entrance and went over to a fire truck to get a stretcher. He went back inside, and presently, together with another fireman, emerged with the stretcher opened and the body of a man on it.

It turned out that the occupant of the house, who lived alone, had dropped a lighted cigarette into an up-holstered chair, which had begun to smolder. Because the windows and doors of the house were shut tightly against the cold, a shortage of fresh air had kept the chair from bursting into flame. Eventually the smoke had asphyxiated him. The occupant was known to do a great deal of drinking, and the firemen found an open whiskey bottle on a sideboard and a glass next to the chair.

An ambulance was summoned, while firemen, using oxygen, attempted resuscitation, but he was too far gone. The smoldering upholstery had also charred his body. Meanwhile firemen began dragging out pieces of the chair. There was a burnt smell over everything. I watched the proceedings for a while longer, until one of the fire trucks departed, then drove back to the newsroom in Hackensack and wrote my story.

The following morning when I stopped by the town manager's office it was to find that a considerable controversy had erupted. It seems that the fire chief had on past occasions complained that when telephone calls had come in that might indicate the possibility of fire, the police were remiss in not notifying the fire department before proceeding to the scene themselves to investigate. The chief now charged that when the police sergeant had received the call from the next-door neighbor the previous evening, he should at once have informed the fire department, and only then gone to the address in question.

The town manager scheduled a public hearing on what had happened. I went by to see the fire chief and got a statement from him, then checked with the sergeant, who of course insisted that nothing about the telephone message had indicated that fire was involved. In my story I described the scene both at police headquarters when the call came in and at the house when the sergeant got there. I reported what the next-door neighbor had told me, which was that "something just seemed wrong, I couldn't tell what." The articles I wrote prior to the hearing were prominently featured in the newspaper, and the town manager half-jokingly accused me of "trying my case in advance." He conceded, however, that having been present at the scene I was only reporting what I had actually observed.

That I had interviewed the next-door neighbor before there had been any indication of a controversy, had taken notes on what he said, with no mention made on his part of anything suggesting the likelihood of fire, and had reported as much in print, made it necessary at the hearing for the fire chief to prove what he could not possibly prove. After the claims of both sides had been aired the manager dismissed the inquiry, declaring that no negligence had been demonstrated in the police department's handling of the incident.

"Just the same," he told me when I talked with him the next day, "I'd like to have heard exactly what the man said when he called."

My role in the episode did no harm whatever to my subsequent relations with the Teaneck police department. Thereafter not only the sergeant who had gone to the scene but the chief of police and everyone else at police headquarters went out of their way to make sure that I knew everything that was going on in town. Several times the sergeant called me at the office to alert me to possible stories.

As for the fire department chief and his cohorts, quite the reverse was true. Henceforth the firefighters answered factual questions put directly to them by me, but volunteered nothing. But since the police responded to all fires and knew whenever one took place, if it was necessary to be in the bad graces of either side, the hook-and-ladder boys were by all means the preferable candidate.

The town manager of Teaneck, Paul A. Volcker, was in his middle years and known in municipal administrative affairs through the country. (Many years later his son was to become famous as chairman of the Federal Reserve Board.) The town, which used the managerial system with an appointed manager and an elected council, was something of a showcase in governmental circles. I liked Volcker, who was candid and informative about town affairs, and he once paid me a compliment—which, in view of what I was then engaged in doing, may not have been so complimentary after all.

The judge of Teaneck's municipal court, a man

named John D. Draney, was noted for the severity with which he handed out penalties to nonresident motorists for violating the speed laws or for reckless driving along the several highways that led through Teaneck, which were heavily traveled by commuters between towns in northern New Jersey and the George Washington Bridge crossing the Hudson River. When time came around for the judge's reappointment for another two-year term, one of the elected town councilmen cut loose with a vehement attack on him, declaring that Teaneck had a deservedly bad name for the unduly steep fines and, in the absence of payment, stays in jail that the judge exacted. Enforcement of the law was one thing, and Draconian harshness quite another, he declared; it was time to get a new and more humane judge.

The other members of the council came to the judge's defense. One after another they praised his impartiality, his rigorous but evenhanded jurisprudence, his refusal to allow influence, political connections, or personal considerations to interfere with the workings of the law. As for his giving the town a reputation for stern enforcement of its traffic laws, one councilman declared that he was quite content for Teaneck to possess such a reputation, and the more people driving through town who knew about it, the better. When the vote was taken, it was 6–1 in favor of His Honor's reappointment.

What I found impressive was the decisiveness with which all the other members of the council had rejected the attacking councilman's accusations. When I wrote my story about the meeting, the unanimity and enthusiasm of the rebuttal was what I emphasized in my lead paragraph. It appeared on page three of the following day's paper, under a two-column headline.

When next I stopped in at the manager's office, Volcker congratulated me on my handling of the story. It was the first time within his memory, he said, that the attack on the judge, which the councilman in question always made when Draney came up for reappointment, hadn't been splashed all over the front page of the *Record,* with the fact that none of the other council members agreed with the critic given only distinctly subordinate billing. Other than from that particular councilman, he said, there were never any complaints about the judge. Not once had his rulings ever been overturned on appeal. In placing the councilman's attack in proper perspective, Volcker told me, I had shown fairness and given an all-too-rare demonstration of "responsible journalism."

Had I, though? Or had I instead made an editorial judgment, and engaged myself in managing the news, rather than straightforwardly reporting events as they happened? I was employed by the *Record,* not by the town of Teaneck, and although it was certainly none of my role to falsify or misrepresent what had hap-

pened, an elected town councilman *had* publicly attacked a sitting judge's performance, demanding that
he not be reappointed. Wasn't that, and not the response of the other council members to his attack,
where the emphasis had belonged? As a reporter of
news what business of mine was it to think in terms
of "fairness"?

Naturally the town manager was gratified that I
had not written my story in such a way as to emphasize controversy over a town official. But what about
my responsibility to interest the readers of the *Bergen
Record* in what was happening on my news beat? Had
I fulfilled that?

Whatever the pros and cons, in retrospect I came
to think that intense though my journalistic ambitions
might have been at the time, the incident demonstrated a serious limitation to my reportorial capabilities. Here was a story that, without any distortion or
sensationalizing on my part, could legitimately have
been written in a way that would guarantee to get it
on the front page—and instead I had deliberately chosen to write it in such a manner as to ensure its appearance on an inside page. That was no way to get
places in the newspaper business.

Still, my handling of the story of the judge's reappointment did, I think, have something to do with my
getting the jump on another and bigger story. A cou-

ple of weeks afterward, when I made my daily visit to
Volcker's office, he suggested that I pay a call on the
town attorney. Which I did, and was told that the
town of Teaneck was charging a local educational institution, Bergen Junior College, with repeated violations of safety regulations in several of its dormitories.
The college, then a privately operated two-year school
and nowadays the Hackensack-Teaneck campus of
Fairleigh Dickinson University, was, like all other institutions of higher education at the time, crowded
with World War II veterans who were taking advantage of the educational opportunities of the "G.I. Bill
of Rights"—just as I had myself done at the University of Richmond after discharge from the Army the
previous year. To accommodate the throngs of new
students, the college had taken over a number of older
private homes in the area and converted them into
makeshift dormitories, installing multiple bunks in
rooms and in hallways.

The town's inspectors had discovered numerous
violations of safety standards. I was shown a set of
8x10 photographs, which revealed exposed gas fixtures
located on walls next to the upper tiers of double-
decker bunks. A stray kick might easily jar them open,
resulting in asphyxiation, fire, and explosion. There
were other violations as well. The case would come
before the municipal court the following week.

I asked whether I might borrow some of the photographs. "Take them along," the town attorney said. "We don't like to do things this way, but they're forcing our hand." It was a front-page story, with photographs both there and inside the paper, and I had been given an exclusive on it.

It would only be fair to permit the school to present its side of the matter, so after my story appeared I telephoned Bergen Junior College and asked for its president, a man named C. L. Littel. He had no comment to make and declined my request for an interview. Whereupon I wrote a story which opened with the statement that the president "would not comment on" the town's charges against the college.

After I turned it in, Jim Sutphen called me over. "If Littel doesn't want to say anything, then just let him not say anything," he told me. "That's his privilege." In so instructing me, Sutphen was quite right, for in writing what I did I was expressing my pique at the president's unwillingness to talk with me, with the implication that his refusal to do so constituted tacit admission that the town's charges were justified. Which may well have been true—but it was no part of my job to be suggesting it.

At the court session the room was packed. An attorney for the college opened his defense with the assertion that the publicity given to the town's charges had created an atmosphere prejudicial to a fair hearing for his client, and asked for a postponement and change of venue. The judge denied the request. "As for newspaper stories," he declared, "I don't read any of them." After both sides had been heard, he handed down fines to Bergen Junior College for each violation and gave the school a stated deadline within which to remedy them or else face additional penalties.

What is intriguing to me is the difference between the manner in which the newspaper responded to the story then, and what under similar circumstances it would very likely do today. Back in 1947 it would not have occurred to the city editor of the *Bergen Record,* and certainly not to myself, that the paper might undertake an investigative role on its own. That I might myself venture with a staff photographer into the old wooden homes being used as dormitories and look around, interview students living in them, find out how much the students and the U.S. Veterans Administration were being charged for dormitory space, inspect other facilities in the dormitories to see how well they were maintained, check earlier records to see whether the college had been guilty of any safety violations in years past, look up property records to learn when and from whom the houses had been purchased and the prices paid for them, examine the property valuations, check the school's tax returns, look into the president's previous history, and the like—nothing of the sort crossed my mind. Nor did the city editor propose that I look any further into the matter.

In general, what is now known as "investigative reporting," in which reporters are assigned to undertake sustained investigations of possible governmental and corporate misconduct, was not what newspapers then did, and certainly not local newspapers like the *Bergen Record*. A newspaper might offer background material, but it was up to district attorneys and prosecutors to look beyond the publicly reported facts. We reported the news; we didn't prosecute cases.

The value of investigative reporting to the welfare of the Republic has been demonstrated often enough. It was the *Washington Post,* not the networks, that uncovered and developed the fact of the Nixon White House cover-up. The television networks portrayed the drama of the Senate hearings, but without what was being turned up daily by print journalism there would have been no televised hearings with congressional committees asking questions. Repeatedly in recent decades investigative reporting by the press has uncovered stories that have revealed graft, corruption, and mismanagement at various levels. All things considered, we are the better off for it.

Even so, I think of the way that the city editor of

the *Record* intervened to prevent me from leading off my follow-up story with the refusal of the president of the junior college to comment on the charges of safety violations: "If Littel doesn't want to say anything, then just let him not say anything." I was on to a good story, and as a reporter I wanted mightily to keep it going. Because I was annoyed at the president's unwillingness to talk with me, I was ready to imply in print that his silence constituted tacit admission of the town's accusations, which whether true or not was inference on my part, not fact. To publish my story as I first wrote it would have been prejudicial to the college's defense, and much though Jim Sutphen may have wanted his paper to publish the news, journalistic ethics mattered to him.

It is just there that today's investigative journalism can and too often does run into trouble. Once hot on the trail of a story, and having turned up newsworthy material, a newspaper wants to keep the story going, and all too often it is willing to do so at the expense of fairness. Invasion of privacy, guilt by association, unwarranted inference, unfounded rumor, unjustified intrusion—in the eagerness to dig up and publish new angles to an ongoing story, the working press has shown itself capable of all these and more.

No small part of the blame for the abuses of investigative journalistic techniques must be ascribed to the pressure to compete with the TV tube. I will say this much for television news, however: For reasons having nothing whatever to do with a desire for fair play, had television news existed back in 1947 it would never have been guilty of the particular injustice that I had been about to perpetrate. For if the junior college president declined to reply to the charges being brought by the town, then as far as television was concerned it would simply be a non-event. Only what could be actually pictured on a television screen would be deemed newsworthy.

As for whether Bergen Junior College eventually removed all the offending gas fixtures from the walls of the makeshift dormitories, and otherwise got itself back into the good graces of the Teaneck town authorities, and if so how long it took to do so, I never found out. For not too long after that I departed from the scene of the crime.

I had come up from Virginia to work on a newspaper in New Jersey because my fiancée lived there. Not long after the judge handed down his verdict in the trial, I too received an adverse verdict. Our engagement to be married was canceled. There was nothing to keep me in the area any longer, so I lost no time in giving Jim Sutphen and the *Bergen Record* notice of my intention to head back south. Sutphen assured me that he could understand my desire to "make a clean break of it," as he put it. "All I can do is to buy you a beer," he told me. I introduced my replacement on the beat to the various civic officials in Teaneck, including the fire chief, who I am sure was not unhappy to see me depart.

After the first excitement of being a full-time newspaper reporter and covering fires, bus wrecks, and the like had worn off, I had not enjoyed living in New Jersey and covering municipal developments in the town of Teaneck. Except for my fall and winter in the Army at Yale it was the first time I had ever lived outside of the South. My trip north, I thought, had been a kind of expedition, an invasion almost—to make a career for myself as a newspaperman, to be engaged and to marry and settle down. And I had failed, been defeated—not, to be sure, in my newspaper career, but in the engagement to be married. It had not worked out.

A few days later I took the train at Penn Station in New York City down to Washington, and there transferred to a Richmond-bound train. Several hours later, on an evening in late February of 1947, I found myself, at age twenty-three, seated in an overheated day coach somewhere between Fredericksburg and Richmond, waiting in the winter darkness about a mile north of a railroad junction at Doswell, Va., where a freight train had jumped the tracks and was totally blocking the main line. It would probably be several hours, a trainman said, before the rails were cleared sufficiently for our train to resume its journey.

The episode seemed painfully appropriate. Like the freight train, I too had been derailed. And although I did not then realize it, not again would I ever set forth from a newsroom in search of a story. I was by no means finished with newspaper work yet, but my brief career as a news reporter—some six months—was done. Meanwhile I waited for the tracks to be cleared of obstructions so that I could resume my journey.

\#   \#   \#

3

A TERM AS CITY EDITOR

Sometime after midnight the tracks were cleared and my train continued on to Richmond. A few days later I rode an Atlantic Coast Line train down to Charleston, where I had grown up and where there was a possible opening on the staff of the morning paper, the *News and Courier*. More than anywhere else, Charleston was where I wanted to work. Nothing was finally forthcoming, however. In Columbia, a hundred miles upstate, I was offered a job on the morning paper, the *State,* but at a salary so small that I knew I could never get by on it.

Returning to Richmond, I learned that there were positions open in Lynchburg and Staunton. I talked with the people in Lynchburg, where a college friend had arranged an interview for me, then rode the bus across the Blue Ridge Mountains to Staunton, in the Shenandoah Valley. The offices of the *News-Leader* and *Evening Leader* were located in an old building with a plate-glass show window, like a retail store. The publisher had already telephoned the persons whose names I had given as references, and was prepared to offer me a job as city editor of the morning paper at a salary of $50 a week—$12 more than I had received in New Jersey.

I agreed to let the publisher know within a few days whether I would take the job, and set out for a walk around downtown Staunton. It was a cold day in late February, with snow a half-foot deep on the ground, a gray sky in the process of clearing up and only beginning to show patches of blue, and a brisk wind that drove granules of snow along the sidewalks. A small city, population about 14,000, Staunton seemed to me to have more of a western than a southern look. The streets, storefronts, and buildings, some of them with towers and cupolas, had a late-nineteenth-century appearance.

The prospect of becoming a city editor was formidable to contemplate. As a reporter in New Jersey, instead of going to my room and to bed after turning in my stories, I frequently helped the night city editor edit and write headlines for stories by the newspaper's numerous correspondents. It was no part of my job; I simply enjoyed doing it. Whatever was involved with getting out a daily newspaper interested me. But to direct a news staff, edit copy, write headlines, and lay out pages—I had assumed that it would be years before I could attain so lofty an eminence. It was true that the *Staunton News-Leader* was a very small paper, with the news staff consisting of a single reporter, along with a part-time sportswriter who was also city editor of the afternoon paper, and a part-time society editor. I would also select and edit the wire news off the Associated Press teletype, edit the copy sent in by rural correspondents, prepare the sports page—in short, do everything except write the local news and the editorials. So it would not exactly be big-time journalism. Still, I would be responsible for getting out a daily newspaper, however small—and this after a mere six months as a reporter.

On the Monday morning following, with suitcase and portable typewriter in hand, I boarded C&O train No. 5, the Sportsman, at the Main Street Station in Richmond. En route to Staunton, a three-hour trip, I read a book entitled *Editing the Small City Daily.*

The Leader Papers of Staunton—pronounced Stanton—were owned by the Opie family. The publisher, E. Walton Opie, who was editor of the morning paper, had commanded a brigade of the 29th Infantry Division in World War II during its training period but, as happened quite often with National Guard units, had been replaced before the division went overseas, and retired from the Army with the rank of major general. His older brother, Hierome Opie, had been a brigadier general in World War I and had edited the *Evening Leader* until his death in the late 1930s. Hierome's son, also named Hierome, who was assistant publisher, had been a Marine major in World War II. Later at the public library I found a Civil War memoir written by the Opie who had founded the newspapers, and who had been a Confederate cavalry trooper.

Despite their martial tradition, they were by no means authoritarian in their way of operating their newspapers, as I soon found out. Those who did their job competently were left alone to do it. The sole exception was Walton Opie's cousin, Mrs. Green, who functioned as treasurer and dispenser of funds, and whose husband had been business manager until his death several years previously.

Mrs. Green, who was endowed with an oversupply of energy, no longer possessed the appropriate means to expend it. So she was into everything. She lived approximately a mile from the office, and in the evening she was on the telephone at the slightest excuse. Whenever the fire alarm sounded and fire trucks left the station with sirens sounding, within a half-minute's time the telephone would ring. "That'll be Mrs. Green," the reporter would remark. "There's a fire alarm," we were informed, as if the noise could not be heard all over town and the fire station were not located a couple of blocks from the office. It soon became all I could do to keep from responding with "I'm glad you told me, because otherwise I might have thought it was an air raid."

My counterpart on the afternoon paper, Jimmy Thacker, told me that the way to handle Mrs. Green was to ignore her. Once I began doing this and she realized it, I received glacial looks whenever I passed by her desk en route to and from the newsroom, but the attempts at superintendence ceased.

Staunton was an older city, dating to well before the Civil War. It was the trading center for the mid–Shenandoah Valley area, and within its precincts were Mary Baldwin College for Women, Staunton Military Academy, the Virginia School for the Deaf and Blind, and the Western Virginia Mental Hospital. The city had no industries to speak of, unlike Waynesboro, fifteen miles to the east, whose daily paper was the Leader Papers' chief rival for circulation in Augusta County. Where Waynesboro was *nouveau riche* and brash, Staunton was Old Money and conservative.

Social status was arranged roughly along lines of

religious affiliation. One of my jobs was to prepare the church page, which ran in Friday morning's paper and involved editing the schedules of forthcoming religious services and activities for consistency of style. It was possible to identify the status of a given church in the local social hierarchy by the appearance and wording of its weekly announcement schedule. These were submitted each week by the churches, and they ranged from neatly typed notices from the larger and more respectable churches to some written in pencil on ruled tablet paper and even on kraft wrapping paper.

As in all southern cities, the Episcopalians occupied the social summit, with the Presbyterians either sharing hegemony or a trifle below, depending upon individual families. The Opies were Episcopalians. The Methodists constituted the middle echelon; in Virginia terms they were "good people" rather than "of good family," and their daughters did not make debuts. The affable and much-liked editor of the *Evening Leader,* Lewis Knowles, was a Methodist. Next came the Baptists, who in their various churches ranged from something equal to Methodist probity on down to various degrees of Hard-Shell fundamentalism.

The Roman Catholics and Jews, who were not numerous, were largely outside the social establishment but contributed some of the community's influential citizens. There was a synagogue in town, which wrote to invite me to attend services. I should have liked to accept, since I might thereby meet some girls, but I worked six nights a week and was free only on Sunday evenings. (In point of fact I lived in Staunton for close to a year and a half, and during that time the only young women I ever came to know worked on the newspaper.)

Also on the scene, though mostly rural rather than living in Staunton itself, were the numerous congregations of the Church of the Brethren, a German sect whose members were distributed throughout the Shenandoah Valley. Farther to the north they were known as Dunkards and Pennsylvania Dutch. Within their ranks were various strata and degrees of orthodoxy, including fundamentalist enclaves whose women wore bonnets and whose men dressed in black and did not drive automobiles or trucks.

Finally, of course, were the blacks. There had been relatively few slaves in the Shenandoah Valley before the Civil War, and the black population was small in comparison with that east of the Blue Ridge. As was true everywhere in Virginia, racial segregation was massive and total.

On one occasion I received a demonstration of the sociability and worldly sophistication of the Episcopal church in Virginia, where it had been flourishing for

more than three centuries and had largely sidestepped
the Puritanical rigors of what in colonial days were
termed the Dissenting churches.

There were two Episcopal churches in Staunton.
The rector of Emmanuel Church was a older man of
conservative theological and civic attitudes, while a
younger man whose views and ways of going about
his work were considerably more adventurous presided
at Trinity Church. Not surprisingly, a decade later
when the controversy over racial integration in public
education became a burning issue in Virginia and the
dominant Democratic Organization controlled by U.S.
Senator Harry F. Byrd sought to shut down the public
schools rather than desegregate them, it was the
younger man, Carroll Brooke, by then a diocesan suf-
fragan bishop, who took an active part in opposing
Massive Resistance and keeping the schools open.

That autumn there was a widely attended fair out
at the fairgrounds, of which one feature was a series of
trotting races. There was no parimutuel betting,
though certainly money did change hands. Because
the races were held in the early afternoon before my
editing routine began, I went out to watch and to
write an account for the morning paper. The facilities
for the judges and the press were located in a raised,
gazebolike wooden structure, topped by a cupola, located in the infield opposite the grandstand and over-

looking the finish line. I introduced myself to the judges and sat down to observe.

Presently the young rector of Trinity Episcopal Church came strolling across the track and over to the judges' platform. As he climbed the stairs and entered the room the judges were debating who was to serve as timer.

"Would you be willing to handle the watch, Pastor Brooke?" someone asked.

"Sure," he replied, taking the proffered stopwatch. "Where's the quarter pole?"

After a week of working on the desk of the *Evening Leader* while Jimmy Thacker, who was normally its city editor, handled the *News-Leader* desk, I was ready to take over as city editor of the morning paper. The *News-Leader* had a circulation of about 7,500 copies, the majority of it rural, while that of the *Evening Leader* was about 4,000, mainly within Staunton itself. There was relatively little overlap; at most a thousand persons were subscribers to both papers. What this meant was that stories appearing in one paper could be reused in the other, and one of my first tasks each day was to mark a copy of the afternoon paper to indicate what type might be picked up, generally local news of lesser importance such as civic club meetings. Each day the advertising department would make up a

dummy indicating where the advertisements were to
be placed throughout the paper, and what space remained for news. Some of the inside pages, containing
mostly advertising, were locked up earlier in the day,
with feature copy and rural correspondence without a
particular time requirement used to fill in the leftover
space. Pages with more open space available were held
back, to be completed during the evening. In actual-
ity the only page that was set entirely in fresh type
each evening was the front page. I could jump stories—i.e., move those paragraphs which couldn't be
fitted onto page 1 into such space as was open inside
the paper, usually on pages 2 and 3 and perhaps here
and there on several others, depending upon the advertising. Except for the editorial page, however,
which was proofed by the editor and locked into place
during the day, the inside pages all contained advertisements, and on days when space was tight the job
became one of deciding which news could be left out
of the paper. On rare occasions, when there was so
much breaking news and almost no room inside to
jump stories onto, the total number of pages in the
edition might be increased by two, but this meant
some reshuffling of advertising, and the approval of the
advertising department was required.

There was also a sports page, which however contained some advertisements, and a half-page of society

news. Except for such local sports events as were covered by the city editor of the afternoon paper, who doubled as sportswriter, the responsibility for the choice of stories and the editing of the sports page was mine.

Not so the news of local society, which was handed by the society editor, a Miss Pancake, whom Jimmy Thacker, no admirer of inherited social status, irreverently called Miss Flapjack. She edited her own copy and wrote her own headlines. Miss Pancake was a graduate of Sweet Briar College, and she knew which announcements of engagements, weddings, and receptions were and were not socially Important. The strategic aspects of the local scene were taken very seriously, and, in ways of which I remained ignorant, the length and the placement on the page of society stories reflected that concern. She also held decided opinions about politics and was not loath to air them. The leveling ways of the New Deal and its then-current successor, the Fair Deal, were not to her liking, and she would denounce in impassioned fashion the Truman administration and all its workings.

Being a Democrat of the New Deal/Fair Deal rather than the States' Rights variety myself, I sometimes argued with her, which rendered her rhetoric still more incandescent. "I just wish," she declared in exasperation on one occasion, "that there was still a *real* Democrat around to vote for!"

Like who? I asked.

"Like Woodrow Wilson, that's who!"

Customarily I began my evening's work by marking up a copy of the afternoon paper for carryover items, finding out from the reporter what local stories would be forthcoming, and checking the Associated Press news budget. This last came in on the teletype in the early afternoon, describing the principal stories that would be arriving during the evening. It did not allow for any breaking news that might develop during the evening. Like other small newspapers the *News-Leader* subscribed to a limited Associated Press service called the "T wire." This provided a selection of national, international, state, and sports news sufficient to keep a single teletype machine clicking steadily away, and produced in fact considerably more copy than could be used.

On the basis of what news was known to be forthcoming I made a tentative diagram of the front page, indicating which stories were to appear and in which of the eight columns, and the sizes and varieties of type that were to be used for their headlines. I would then set in to edit copy. The AP teletype news was transmitted entirely in capital letters, which required going through it and underlining those letters which were actually to be capitalized in print. Once a story was edited I wrote a headline on a separate sheet of paper, which depending upon the size of the type and the content of the headline could be an easy or a difficult task.

Inasmuch as the use of linotypes, metal type, and all that these entailed has largely disappeared from newspapers nowadays in favor of computerized photocomposition and paste-up lithography, it may be useful to describe the basic operation of linotypes. They were large keyboard machines containing magazines loaded with type matrices. When a key was touched the appropriate matrix slid down, and when enough were in place to fill out a line, they were tightened by the use of spacebands, and hot lead poured into them. The result was a lead slug, type-high (about .918 inch), with the width and length depending upon the page format and the size of type. Along the top of the slug were the letters, reading backward—thus, a line-o'-type. The slugs were dropped onto a tray, one after another, while a distributor bar reached down, grasped the matrices, and lifted them up to be returned to the magazine for reuse. All was done automatically; the linotype operator needed only to tap the letter and space keys and, when a line was complete, to lift a lever which elevated the row of matrices and activated the casting process. It was many times faster than even the most rapid composition by hand, and the matrices were automatically redistributed while the operator was setting the next line of type.

The more copy that could be edited and set early in the evening, the better, because four linotype machines could produce only so many lines of type, and quite often there were evenings when only three operators might be available for work. The unexpected appearance of a late-breaking story, whether local news or from the Associated Press, could throw everything into disarray, necessitating additional last-minute typesetting, revision of the front-page layout and new headlines, and the frantic moving around of blocks of type.

When the makeup man was ready to begin work on the front page, which was kept for last and was usually about 11 P.M., I went back into the composing room to supervise. Working in accordance with the page diagram, he slid lines of linotype composition from the steel galley trays, on which they had been placed for proofing after being set, onto the heavy steel makeup table with wheels, called a turtle, atop which lay a page-sized steel frame called a chase. Within the chase and below the newspaper nameplate the columns of type had to be placed, and the headlines, which were set into type separately, positioned atop the appropriate stories. Lead slugs and rules were inserted between the columns and between the stories in the columns.

However careful one might be in diagramming a page, the fit could never be exact. It would always be necessary to shorten some stories, either by eliminating paragraphs or by jumping some type onto inside pages. In order for the words to read normally when inked and printed, type was cast with the letters reading backward. To facilitate moving it about in the chase, it was usually worked upside down—i.e., with the top of the page nearest to the makeup man and the bottom farthest away. The trick when making up a page was to learn to read it that way—upside down, with the letters reversed.

On newspapers with unionized shops, there was a sharp division of effort between what editors and printers could do in making up a page. The editor told the printer what he wished done, and the printer moved the type around. For an editorial employee to touch any printing equipment would have brought a shout of "Chapel!" and every printer in the plant would have stopped work. But the composing room of the Staunton papers was nonunion, which meant that I was not barred from moving type around myself, exploring the type trays in long-unused cabinets, setting type, and even using a linotype machine. Ever since I had gone down to a print shop as a high school student to help get out the school newspaper, type, typography, and everything having to do with printing had fascinated me. Now I could indulge my curiosity whenever I wanted.

The personnel of the *Staunton News-Leader*'s composing room were, all in all, a patchy bunch. (Unionized printers would have cost considerably more.) To begin with, the night foreman, who operated one of the linotype machines, was a deaf mute. To communicate with him it was necessary to write out what one wished to say. Another of the linotype operators was given to strong drink, and sometimes came to work incapacitated. One never knew for sure how many linotype machines would be manned that evening. There was a period when for a full week we were without an operator for one of the four machines. Then a white-haired gentleman named McGowan, who lived over in Highland County, was hired to fill the vacancy. A hearty soul in his late sixties or early seventies, to get to and from work each evening he drove fifty-five miles each way across the Shenandoah Mountains.

McGowan had certain ways of spelling and abbreviating that did not accord with normal usage, and when setting type did not hesitate to apply them regardless of how the copy read. Occasional requests that

he reset lines in order to bring the stories he was setting into conformity with those set by the other operators were not at all to his liking. He would do it,
but with commentary. "You young whippersnapper,"
he would declare, "just who do you think you are,
telling me how to spell? Why, I used to set type for
Horace Greeley!" I looked up Greeley's dates. He had
died in 1872, several weeks after his unsuccessful run
for president, which meant that if McGowan had
been, say, eighteen years old during Greeley's last year
as editor of the *New York Tribune,* he would currently
have been ninety-five, which seemed unlikely.

My chief problems, however, came not from linotype operators but the *News-Leader's* makeup man,
Jackson. He was sober and hard-working, and his ha-
bitual mode of operation was Full Speed Ahead. This
sometimes made for imprecision, and he needed to be
watched. More crucially, Jackson was able neither to
read nor to write. He could, with difficulty, identify
individual letters of the alphabet, but complete words
were more than he could handle. For someone
charged with getting blocks of type located in the
proper places within a chase, this could constitute a
handicap.

So long as the newsroom was next door to the
composing room and I could stand next to him and
point to stories needing to be moved about in the

chase, all went reasonably well. A year or so after I began work in Staunton, however, it was decided to expand the business office and move the editorial functions to the second floor, until then used for storage and reachable only via a staircase opening onto the sidewalk next to the front office.

To facilitate the exchange of copy and proof, a copy chute was installed, in the form of a dumb-waiter consisting of a plywood box located within plywood housing. The box could be moved between floors by tugging on a pulley rope. One terminus was placed next to the city desk in the upstairs newsroom, and the other in the composing room directly below it. At each a string of bells was installed, connected to a cord, to be jangled before the box was to be moved up or down and thus alert anyone who might at that moment be reaching into the basket to withdraw his or her hand before it received a blow from the lip of the wooden box.

To use the new copy chute was to place oneself in physical peril. For Jackson, who was habitually in a hurry, could not always remember to jangle the bells before jerking on the pulley rope to retrieve the box from upstairs, and when he did remember he would give the bells a quick jerk with one hand while simultaneously yanking the pulley rope with the other. The result was that until the inhabitants of the newsroom learned to approach the copy chute at all times as if it were an explosive device, there were bruised wrists and fingers and numerous close escapes. Someone, usually myself, might have a hand thrust into the box just as Jackson yanked the pulley rope. Whereupon the would-be user's next word might be "*Ow!*" followed by "Goddammit, you son of a bitch! Ring that bell before you pull the rope!" Jackson was always deeply penitent, but a half-hour later, caught up in the fervor of his work, he would do it again.

For voice communication with the composing room an intercom was installed, with one station on the city editor's desk and the other mounted on a post next to where the pages were made up. The new arrangements posed no great handicap for the afternoon paper's staff, and moreover had the advantage of placing the news staff on a separate floor from Mrs. Green. But at night, with a composing room foreman who could neither speak nor hear and a makeup man unable to read or write, it was otherwise.

If, for example, an important news story, unlisted in the Associated Press's budget and so not previously diagrammed on the layout sheet, were to materialize, meaning that another story would have to be transferred to a place of lesser prominence on the page, it would have been relatively easy to type out a note and convey the information to the composing room. Such a note might read: "*Move TRUMAN PROPOSES from the top of column 4 to the left hand side of the page underneath CITY COUNCIL, and put BERLIN AIRLIFT on the top of column 4. Jump whatever of TRUMAN PROPOSES that won't fit to page 3.*"

That would work fine—during the daytime, with the *Evening Leader's* crew. But at night Jackson would be unable to read any such note, while the composing room foreman was not only deaf but would be too busy setting type to stand over Jackson and direct the transaction.

There were two courses of action possible. One was to leave my desk, go down the stairs and out the door onto the sidewalk, enter the front door, walk back through the business office to the composing room, and there indicate on the chase which stories were to be moved and inserted, and where they were to go. To stop what I was working on every time that a change in makeup was needed, however, was a decided nuisance. In the instance described above I might very likely be at work editing the fast-breaking BERLIN AIRLIFT copy as it arrived in installments on the teletype, underlining the capital letters, inserting subheads, and writing the headline, while downstairs the takes were being set into type as I sent them along.

So I would attempt to communicate with Jackson over the intercom, whereupon the conversation might go something like this:

"Jackson?"

"Yeah?"

"What do you have at the top of column 4?"

(*Lengthy pause*) "T . . . (*pause*) R . . . (*long pause*) U . . . "

"That's it. TRUMAN. Well, move it underneath CITY COUNCIL in column 1. Do you see where I mean?"

(*Another lengthy pause*) "C . . . (*pause*) I . . . T . . . "

And so it went. Moving one story required moving a second, and moving that usually meant moving a third, and so on, until several pages were involved, with each step in the swapping of type having literally to be spelled out. Usually I ended up going downstairs anyway.

Inasmuch as Jackson could not spell words, he was unable to distinguish groups of letters that together made words from others that did not. Because of the way that linotypes functioned, this could be a hazard. If while setting copy linotype operators made mistakes, they were accustomed to drag their fingers down the rows of keys, thereby dropping down enough type matrices to fill out the rest of the faulty line—etaoin-shrdlu, etc.—which could then be cast into a lead slug and discarded while they reset the line correctly. Thus if when beginning the name Eisenhower the operator happened to get an extra *i* into it—Eisien—he would fill out the remainder of the line so that it could be cast and the faulty slug removed. Thus, "Eisienetaoinshrdluetaoinshr."

After setting the line correctly, the operator was supposed to pull the botched line out from the accumulating row of linotype slugs. But the linotype operator sometimes failed to do so, and both the faulty and the corrected line remained in the galley to be inked and proofed. It was then the proofreader's job to spot the wasted line in the galley being read, and mark it to be removed.

Working at a desk across from mine in the newsroom each evening was the *News-Leader*'s sole proofreader, Mr. Sheets, a man in his seventies, of dignified mien and a totally bald pate with a single large bump to one side of it. He was a widower, with his children long since grown up and moved away, and lived in a room at the YMCA. A good-hearted old gentleman, as a proofreader Mr. Sheets had one handicap: a pronounced facial tic. Whenever his head gave a twitch, as several times each minute it did, he would skip several lines of proof.

The result was that one might be reading along in a story and suddenly come upon "Eisienetaoinshrdluetaoinshr," either instead of or in addition to the corrected line. If this was on the front page, we usually caught it before the edition went to press, but if on an inside page it might not be caught at all, because Jackson, in a hurry as always, would not have noticed the botched line before turning the page over to the press crew for stereotyping and mounting on the press.

On at least one occasion, however, Jackson did find an apparently botched line and removed it. For Groundhog Day I wrote a piece in which a groundhog, irked at being roused from its rest, was supposedly being queried on various matters of local import. A half-dozen or so questions were asked, after which there followed a sentence of which random marks of punctuation were used to indicate profanity. These happened to constitute the major part of a linotype slug: "To all these queries, the groundhog replied: '!!!!★$(★★)(&##@@!!!! ★%$★%#&&!!'"

As the page was about to be borne off for stereotyping, the eagle-eyed Jackson spotted what was surely a botched line of type. Upon which he quickly unlocked the chase, removed the offending slug, inserted a blank slug at the bottom of the story to make up for the line that had been lost, retightened the page, and sent it on to be printed.

In retrospect, I realized that his doing this was fated and inevitable. A phenomenon that I have observed not a few times over the years is that the one thing that can under no circumstances be gotten into the

columns of a newspaper is an *intentional* spelling error
(I emphasize the qualifier). At some point on the way
to the pressroom, it is bound to be noticed and corrected. (Nowadays most newspapers no longer employ
proofreaders, because the changed process of
photocomposition and computerized editing requires
numerous scannings of copy before it goes to press.
Even so, typos can creep in. As Isaac Watts said of bears
and lions growling and fighting, 'tis their nature to.)

When the front page was at last ready, with all stories
properly in place, a proof of it had to be pulled and
checked closely by everyone available in the newsroom—i.e., the city editor, the reporter, and the proofreader. Only then, after being read and—one hoped—
all remaining typographical errors caught, could the
page be rolled back into the stereotyping room for a
papier-mâché mat to be made of it. The mat then
went into a casting mold which converted it into a
metallic half-cylinder for mounting upon the presses.
The Leader Papers' press, which I was told had once
belonged to the *Nashville Tennessean* back in the days
of the spectacular publisher-politico-financier Colonel
Luke Lea, was capable of producing approximately
14,000 copies an hour of an edition consisting of one
twelve-page or two eight-page sections.

By the time that the front page was locked up and

proofed, it was often after 1 A.M. Before and afterward I worked at my desk editing copy from the paper's rural correspondents, which was used on inside pages as space permitted, and selecting and editing features from AP Newsfeatures, the National Geographic Society, and other such which could be used as filler copy.

Whenever possible I tried to have at least one illustration on the front page. The Leader Papers did not have a staff photographer, for the reason that they did not have any engraving facilities. Each day, however, AP Newsfeatures provided a selection of photo mats for casting into lead, which usually arrived one day after being mailed. The trick was to select photos of events which remained in the news beyond the first day, and adapt the captions to the next day's story. If, for example, there were an airplane crash, and a photo mat of the wreckage arrived in the mail the day following, it could be used to illustrate a story on the aftermath of the wreck and the investigation into its cause.

Front-page layout intrigued me. I ordered a couple of books on page design and adapted some of the examples to our typography. I made diagrams of other newspapers' front pages that I thought interesting, and tried them out on our front page. Frequently this involved using streamer headlines and having the opening paragraphs of lead stories set in two-column width and in type that was larger than the *News-Leader*'s customary body type. There were days when the front page of our little 7,500-circulation paper looked as gaudy as that of any metropolitan daily battling for enhanced newsstand sales. Modifications to such designs, of course, were always necessary, because the *News-Leader*'s typographical resources were restricted, and there was also the difficulty that limited space was available inside the paper. So it was necessary to crowd a great deal of news onto the front page, which gave it a cluttered appearance.

When I first joined the *Staunton News-Leader* the sole reporter was a local girl, a graduate of Mary Baldwin College. A very capable young woman, she had developed excellent relations with the city and state police, the municipal and the Augusta County government, and the courts. Then she left to take a job with the Federal Bureau of Investigation. Thereafter came a succession of reporters, each of whom had to learn the local situation anew. There was a young war widow from Mississippi, a very fine person. She was followed by a man from Washington, D.C., who was competent at the work but quit after several weeks, remaining in town as an *Encyclopaedia Britannica* salesman.

His successor as a reporter was a young woman who was on the timid side, yet who, paradoxically, seemed capable of conducting her interrogation of municipal officials and law officers in such a way as to incur much resistance. One evening, a few weeks after she began work, she came in after a stop at police headquarters to report that there had been an automobile accident, but that the officer who had gone to the scene had refused to give her any details and had spoken very harshly to her.

It was a light night for news, I had completed editing all the telegraph and local copy, and the police station was just around the corner from the newspaper offices. I decided to walk over there, explain to the officer that the reporter was new on the job and had meant no harm, and get the information on the accident. When I approached the officer in question, however, he began shouting that he was not going to talk about what had happened, and stormed out of the squad room.

I went back to the office and wrote a brief story noting that an accident had occurred, but declaring that the officer, whose name I gave, had refused to divulge any information to the *News-Leader*'s reporter. I quoted him as having shouted that "I don't want to hear anything more about it!" Then I put a headline on the story reading something like "POLICE WON'T TELL ABOUT AUTO CRASH" and ran the story in boldface type inside a ruled box on the front page.

It got results—and fast. The chief of police came

hustling over to see General Opie. Called into his office, I told them what had happened. The chief expressed his regret over what he described as "the misunderstanding." The officer in question, he explained, had not known who I was, or understood what I had wanted. All ended amicably. After the chief had departed the General told me that what I should probably have done was to have telephoned the desk sergeant when I got back to the office, told him what I intended to write, and given him a chance to rectify matters. "Then if they won't cooperate, we'll just smoke 'em out," he said. In any event, our reporter encountered no more difficulty thereafter in getting details of accidents and arrests from the Staunton police department.

There was one occasion, however, when the General did find it necessary to curb my journalistic zeal. It was the custom of the local undertaking parlors to prepare obituary notices of their clients for use in the newspaper. I had written and rewritten numerous obituaries in New Jersey, and I proceeded to edit them in the same way for the *News-Leader,* including all the biographical material provided but eliminating expressions of opinion. In particular, a local mortician was given to statements such as "entered into eternal rest in the bosom of the Almighty" and "he was a loving father and devoted, faithful husband" and "she will be deeply missed by all who knew and cherished her" and the like. After a few weeks of having all such comments excised from his obituaries he protested to the publisher.

General Opie asked me why the obituary copy was being so severely amputated. I was only removing expressions of opinion, I said, on the theory that if the statements were valid, the deceased's family and friends did not have to be told so, and if they were untrue, no one was going to believe them anyway.

The General laughed. "You remind me of the story of the old mountaineer who died," he said. "He was a crook, a deadbeat, he drank like a fish, he was always getting into fights, he'd been in jail half a dozen times, and was generally a worthless human being. So for the graveside service the preacher was hard put to think of anything good to say about him. But finally he managed to come up with something about him loving his wife and his children, and he did as much along that line as he possibly could.

"So, after the burial one of the men who knew the deceased well turned to the man next to him and said, 'Well, all I got to say is, if Bill Jones goes to heaven, I'll kiss the devil's ass!'"

It would not do, however, to apply rigid news standards to the death notices, he said; that was not how the Leader Papers handled obituaries. "Just let them say what they want, as long as they don't get too flowery." Lewis Knowles had also been approached, and he told me the same thing. "The families will clip out the obituaries and paste them in the family Bible," he said. I was not convinced, but I did my best thereafter to refrain from working over the obituary notices other than for spelling.

Nowadays no such problems arise on most newspapers, because except in the instance of prominent persons, whose deaths are considered news and are handled as such, obituaries are printed as paid notices, to be published as submitted, in whatever length and including whatever editorial commentary desired, however flowery, at so much per line.

In Virginia, elections for state and local offices were held in odd-numbered years, and in the autumn of my first year in Staunton there were contests for various offices, including state senator and delegates and county sheriff. The Leader Papers were engaged in a running feud with the incumbent sheriff of Augusta County, a man named Wilkerson. It was said to have started during the war when Mr. and Mrs. Green were returning home late on a Saturday night after attending a football game in Lexington, fifty miles south of Staunton, and were stopped and given a speeding ticket. One thing led to another, and a full-fledged vendetta developed, which after the business manager's death continued with unflagging zeal.

On the part of the sheriff, who had been in office for some years and had come to regard the job as his hereditary property, the vendetta took the form of a total lack of cooperation with the newspapers' reporters in securing information about crimes, arrests, auto wrecks, and the like. By law the sheriff's office was obliged to allow its records of arrests and jailings to be examined, but to do this a reporter had to come to the office; no information was ever given out via telephone. At ten or eleven o'clock at night this could be a considerable nuisance.

So when a former Virginia state trooper named Shaver announced that he would be a candidate for the sheriff's job in the fall election, the newspapers were very much on his side. Because the reporters would have to deal with the winner of the election and his staff on a day-by-day basis, I was asked to interview him and write a feature story about his candidacy, which I did.

The weekend preceding the voting, in an editorial appearing in both the Saturday edition of the *Evening Leader* and the Sunday morning *News-Leader,* the papers gave their formal endorsements to a slate of candidates, including Shaver. On election night there was great excitement. Lewis Knowles and the afternoon paper's staff were on hand to help with the coverage. People were assigned to concentrate on various races, while I took care of the teletype news, edited such nonpolitical news as there was, wrote all the headlines, and saw to the page makeup.

By midevening a considerable group had gathered in the business office at the front of the building. There was a definite social dimension to the occasion; Staunton's elite were present in force, with Mrs. Green functioning as hostess. The state senator and the representatives to the Virginia House of Delegates, being members of the Establishment in good standing, were on hand to follow the returns and to receive congratulations. When the successful candidate for sheriff, Shaver, who was not a member, came in to deliver his statement to the newsroom, Mrs. Green shook his hand warmly and expressed her approval of his victory, which in her eyes was neither more nor less than a triumphal vindication of the long-standing feud with the incumbent.

While all this was going on up front in the business office, the editorial staff worked away. We got the morning paper out on schedule, with streamer headlines proclaiming the election results. By the time the proof of the front page was ready for checking, the celebration in the front of the building had ended, the afternoon staff had gone home, and things were back to normal.

Later I was to take part in election nights on several other newspapers, and although the gatherings were less socially structured and more in terms of the newspaper proprietors' political alliances, there was always the same mixture of editorial personnel working away and visitors who otherwise were never seen in newsrooms coming by to mingle with the paper's owners and executives as the returns came in. The excitement intensified as the returns multiplied; no other journalistic occasion was like it. Much the longer part of my life has gone by since I was last part of the operations of a newsroom on election night. It is the only time when I miss being a newspaperman.

After some months on the job I borrowed some money and bought my first automobile. During the war there had been a four-year hiatus in automobile production, and although new cars were now appearing on the market again, used cars were still in very short supply. The one I bought, an eleven-year-old Plymouth coupe, cost $400, or approximately eight weeks of my salary. After that I was no longer confined to downtown Staunton, and on weekends was not dependent upon the bus and the train. I could drive to Richmond, a hundred miles distant, in the very early hours of Sunday morning after I finished work, and return on Monday afternoons. Or I could visit other places and photograph railroads, which was then my hobby.

Having a car enabled me to work on feature stories. The Shenandoah Valley was sheep-raising country, and on one occasion the National Sheep Dog Trials were held six miles from Staunton, near Verona. Before the event I interviewed the tournament officials about what sheep dogs did and how they were trained, and wrote a story about that. The next day I watched as a flock of a half-dozen or so sheep were released into a field, and a dog and its trainer set out to corral them into a penned-in area some distance away. The dogs, border collies with black and white fur, were extremely adept at observing their owners' hand signals and maneuvering the sheep as directed.

Until needed, the sheep to be herded were kept together, a hundred strong, in a roped-off pen behind the grandstand. At one point in the afternoon's proceedings the daily freight train of the Chesapeake Western Railroad, a short line operating between Staunton and Harrisonburg, came rumbling along. There was a grade crossing nearby, and when the locomotive reached a point about fifty yards from it and directly behind where the sheep were being kept, its air horn cut loose with a loud warning *blatt!*

The sheep, which until then had been grazing peacefully, responded as one. *En masse* they bolted in the opposite direction from the train, toward the grandstand area. Some of the dog handlers came running with their dogs to block their flight. At the point where the rope barrier stretched, men, dogs, and sheep

converged. Moving at express-train speed, the sheep
vaulted over both the rope barrier and the heads of
the handlers and sprinted past the grandstand toward
the open pasture and the rolling hills beyond. The proceedings had to be suspended for an hour while dogs
and men joined in rounding up the sheep and herd-
ing them back to the pen.

When Lewis Knowles went away on a week's vacation, General Opie asked me to write the editorials
for the *Evening Leader.* I stayed away from politics,
since the General's views were considerably more
conservative than mine. However, I did write an editorial having to do with southern race relations, which
if read nowadays would seem condescending and even
reactionary but at the time was, for a southern
newspaper, very much on the heretical side. So much
so that the young Episcopal minister, Carroll Brooke,
spied me walking along downtown and called over
from across the street, "Lewis ought to stay on vacation!" I daresay that not many of his parishioners
would have agreed with him.

By the time that I had been city editor for a year,
there was almost nothing having to do with the workings of a daily newspaper that had not in one way or
the other come under my eye, on however small a
scale. Few young journalists had been as directly in-

volved in so many of the various editorial and mechanical operations. The terms on which that familiarity had been gained, however, were those of an almost
total isolation from anyone who could share my professional and intellectual interests, as well as the absence of any tutelage by older, more experienced journalists.

What it came down to was that once I had learned
my job as city editor, I found it increasingly boring.
This was not the fault of the job, any more that of
those I worked for and with. But they had other interests—their families, their friends, their recreations
and other doings, the contexts of their lives as members of a community—while all I had was the
newspaper work itself, which for an unmarried man
just turning twenty-four and with as-yet-untested literary ambitions was not enough.

When not at work I was living virtually a solitary
existence. Never was I invited to anyone's house.
Other than employees of the newspaper I knew no
one in town, and the schedule that I worked made it
next to impossible for me to meet anyone, in particular girls my own age. Monday through Saturday, from
late afternoon until after 1 A.M., I was at my job, with
Sunday my only evening off. Some nights when I finished work, instead of returning to my room and reading myself to sleep, if the weather were mild I walked
over to the railroad station and watched a freight train

come through town. There was one that usually arrived from the west sometime after 2 A.M. Occasionally I even stayed on for the arrival of the westbound F.F.V., a passenger train which stopped in Staunton about three in the morning en route to the Midwest. There was nothing else to do but go back to my room and read.

One of my jobs was to serve as stringer for the Richmond bureau of the Associated Press. When there was a story that was of potential interest beyond Staunton and Augusta County, I called it in or sent it over the AP teletype. In the spring of 1948 a vacancy occurred on the AP staff, and I was offered a job. Although I would have to take a sizable cut in salary, I did not hesitate to accept.

I was offered a raise—I had received one earlier—if I would stay on, but my mind was made up. I remained in Staunton for several more weeks to instruct my successor in the workings of the job, then loaded my belongings into my car and left for Richmond. My tenure as a city editor was done.

That was fifty-two years ago. The technical knowledge I gained as city editor of a small city daily has largely been rendered obsolete. On newspapers in the 1940s, printing was being done much as Johannes Gutenberg had done it at Mainz in the fifteenth century. The process had been speeded up considerably; that was all.

And William Caslon or Benjamin Franklin could have walked into the composing room of the *Staunton News-Leader,* rolled up his sleeves, and made up the front page without undue difficulty. Today, a half-century later, the development of photocomposition, offset lithography, and computerized technology has changed everything. Ink, newsprint, and rotary presses are still employed; but the similarity stops there.

As for the editorial skills—handling copy, writing headlines, designing page layouts—these remain usable. The discipline of working toward a set, inescapable deadline has proved very valuable. One does the very best that one can do with an assignment, then must turn it loose and go on to something else. But there are also liabilities. It is not always either possible or desirable to try to phrase everything one wishes to say so that it can be made immediately available to a newspaper reader.

What as a writer and reader I admire most of all is the perception and the delineation of complexity. It took me a while to begin to realize this, and at the time that I left Staunton it did not occur to me, not even remotely, that what I was looking for might not appropriately be found in a newsroom at all.

#   #   #

4

THE ASSOCIATED PRESS; OR, REWRITING MY OWN REWRITES

The newspaper job that for the first time caused me to question whether I was meant to be a journalist was with the Associated Press. Until then, although certainly there had been aspects of newspaper work that I had not cared for, I had always assumed that the kind of writing that I wished to do and was best qualified to do could be accomplished for newspapers. It was a matter of finding, or growing into, the right job in the right place, I thought. But after no more than a few months of working for the AP in Richmond, I began doing what I had never before done—which was, to think of daily journalism not as a career objective in itself, but instead as a way of earning a living while doing the kind of writing I most wanted to do on my own time. It took a while for the implications of that discovery to make themselves fully realized, but working for the AP was where it began.

I should make it clear at once that I was by no means sure what that more-favored sort of writing was to be. I had in mind writing fiction; supposedly that was to be it. Yet although I was enthralled by certain writers of fiction, notably Thomas Wolfe, and wished to emulate them, I was not really yearning to tell stories as such. It would be misleading, too, to describe myself as engaged in groping for an appropriate literary voice and form, in the way that Wolfe, to use him as an example, spent a half-dozen or so years attempting to write plays before discovering that prose fiction was his milieu. If I came to believe that novels were what I wanted to learn how to write, then this was true only in the abstract, as a vague idea that presented itself as the occasion for literary "creativity," whatever that was.

The Wolfe novels were of central importance to me as a young man, far more than in later years I find it easy to explain. What I most liked about them was the example they offered for the emotional rehearsing of one's own youthful experience. As a reader I identified with Thomas Wolfe the author as he engaged in the act of writing about his life in and through his auto-biographical protagonist. I mean this in the most literal sense. That Wolfe wrote in the third person but really meant the first person singular, and that the reader was made to take part in the seeming objectivity of what was actually ferociously subjective, was vital to the reader's involvement. (I did not then know that Wolfe *had* in fact written *Of Time and the River* in the first person, only to have his editor change it from "I" to "he.")

So-called autobiographical fiction, as I came to realize in later years, is not an aspect of subject matter as such, but of the relationship between the subject matter and the way that the author tells about it. "I celebrate myself, and sing myself," begins *Leaves of Grass;* yet the "I" and the "myself" are not the autobiographical Walt Whitman. When we have finished reading that long and often magnificent piece of inspired parthumbuggery we scarcely know much more about the poet's actual life than at the outset. He comes from New York City and he believes in democracy; that is all. Not so with Wolfe; the character whose experience is being presented and the voice of the author are for all intents and purposes one and the same—the author is older, but not greatly so. What I coveted was the opportunity to get some of my own emotions into what I wrote—not, of course, directly, but something more than the mere repetition of factual data.

What, however, did writing for the Associated Press have to do with that? It had nothing whatever to do with it, and *that* was the point. In effect I had moved into a situation in which the kind of writing I was expected to do was at a 180° remove from anything connected with my own feelings. I might as readily have turned into a robot compiling financial statistics; there was *nothing* about what I now did that provided for anything other than routine competence in language. The very thought of stylistic concerns was laughable.

How I could have failed so totally to understand what I was getting myself into seems, with even a modicum of hindsight, staggeringly obtuse on my part. I can only account for it by the intensity of my desire to move on from the journalistic backwater in which I had been living and working, and to become part of an organization that, in theory at least, was directly concerned with covering the news all over the nation and the world. I saw the move as the opening up of a window of opportunity. When I perceived that it wasn't, the realization was devastating. For being a staff writer for the AP had seemed to me, when a youth growing up with newspapering ambitions, to be exciting and even glamorous. As perhaps it could be, but certainly not in a small regional bureau in Richmond, Virginia.

The bare facts of the new job were as follows. As with my previous position as city editor of the *Staunton News-Leader,* I reported for duty in the late afternoon—though I now worked five nights a week, not six. The bureau's offices were located in the Richmond Newspapers building, on the same floor with the newsrooms of the *Times-Dispatch* and the *News-Leader.* Carbon copies of the news stories written by the reporters on those newspapers were turned over to the AP. It was my job, as "night state editor" (everybody was an editor of some kind), to rewrite those of more than local importance to be moved via teletype to other newspapers in the state of Virginia. Very occasionally a story was of sufficient moment to be sent out over the national AP news wire. During the evening, stringers from various newspapers throughout the state also called in, just as I had done while in Staunton, with stories to be taken down over the telephone.

All these stories were designed to appear in the next morning's newspapers. Not a spark of imagination or originality was involved on my part; all that I did was to rewrite what others had already written. Not only that, but later in the evening I was expected to rewrite my own rewrites for the early editions of the next afternoon's papers, saying whatever had already been said twice a little differently so that it would not constitute a word-for-word repeat of my first rewriting.

When I accepted the job I had known that I would be expected to do some rewriting. What I had not expected, however, was to discover that except when the state legislature was in session, only a single member of the bureau's staff was ever assigned to cover stories himself, instead of rewriting the stories provided by the two Richmond newspapers. There were staff members who had been with the Richmond bureau for several years and who were never sent out of the office to develop stories. Either they did what I was doing or else they "filed the wire," which consisted of deciding which stories should be sent out to member newspapers by teletype, and to what length and in what order.

Very occasionally someone might be dispatched elsewhere in the state to cover a sporting event that for one reason or another no member newspaper was covering. But I soon learned that years would have to elapse before I might aspire to the honor and excitement of covering, say, the Virginia state golf tournament.

As for the notion that by working for the AP in Richmond I would be a staff member of a worldwide press organization, with opportunities after a few years to move on to Washington or New York City or the like, I discovered that within living memory no member of the Richmond bureau staff had ever been transferred elsewhere; there was one man stationed in Washington, but he was on the Richmond staff and his assignment was entirely that of reporting on Virginia matters.

Working with me in the Richmond bureau was a
college friend, Paul Duke. Some years afterward, Paul
gave the bureau chief an ultimatum: either transfer
him to the Washington bureau or he would leave the
Associated Press. Reluctantly the bureau chief
arranged the transfer. Paul later went from the AP to
the *Wall Street Journal,* then to NBC News, and finally
to WETA-TV, where he developed *Washington Week in
Review* for PBS. If he had not insisted, he would
doubtless have finished up his career in Richmond.

The Richmond bureau took its character from the
personality of the bureau chief, and the bureau chief
was one of the most deadly dull writers I have ever
known. He did not in truth do much writing, but
what he did was pedestrian stuff even for routine factual journalism. When I first read some of his copy I
was astounded. His paragraphs, even including his
leads, consisted of one short declarative sentence after
the other, three or four to the paragraph, and were in-
nocent of the slightest awareness that it was possible to
use language to say something *well.*

In point of fact there were on the staff of the Richmond bureau several excellent journalists in addition
to Duke, but the bureau chief could no more have
identified the merits of their prose as against that of
the most humdrum hacks on his staff than he could
have distinguished between the flavors of hyssop and
oolong teas.

It was not long after I began work for the AP that I realized that the bureau chief had taken advantage of my naïveté to get by with paying me a minimum salary. Because I had been working as a newspaperman for less than two full years, he had told me, the AP's contract with the American Newspaper Guild was such that he could pay me only a certain amount. This was a flat-out lie, which I should have spotted. The Guild's contract specified a *minimum* salary; it did not set any maximum figure. So eager was I to join the AP, however, that I did not even question the assertion. Sensing my eagerness, and using the Guild arrangements as an excuse, he offered me a third less money than I was making in Staunton, and jackasslike I accepted the offer. When after a few weeks on the job I was enlightened concerning the deception by a fellow staff member, I was thoroughly disillusioned. It was the first (and the only) time that I was ever dealt with other than honorably by anyone in a position of authority in the field of journalism.

Doubtless the bureau chief's superiors in New York or wherever were gratified at the low budget on which he operated. From that standpoint I assume that he was an ideal choice to head a small regional AP bureau; he kept salaries down to a minimum and served as a kind of punching bag to absorb the complaints of the various Virginia newspapers who were AP members. To keep peace in the family, so to speak, he was willing to sacrifice the self-respect of his own staff members to the complaints, however irrational, of the occasional sorehead among news executives. There was one occasion when I reported a story in a quite straightforward way, only to have the managing editor of the *Roanoke Times,* who was renowned for his irascibility, complain loudly about the bureau's supposed mishandling of the story. To my considerable annoyance, instead of backing up my decision, which I had cleared with the editor who was filing the wire that evening, the bureau chief's only thought was to pacify the managing editor, even to the point of not challenging his highly distorted version of what had happened.

He did not, to be sure, censure either myself or the editor filing the wire. But neither did he come to our defense and make it clear, in the face of what was obviously unjustified and unreasonable criticism, that he stood behind us. No doubt it was easier and more politic to do what he did than to confront the complainant, but it left me with a bad taste in my mouth.

The absence of any opportunity to write stories on my own initiative, and the need to confine what I wrote primarily to revision of others' stories, quickly grew irksome. One of my assignments was to assemble the accounts of Piedmont League baseball games from the stories sent in during the week by the AP member newspapers and prepare a roundup—a review of the progress of the pennant race. Finding a different angle each week for a story that involved no new information whatever, and had to be based entirely on what had already appeared in print, became an exercise in ingenuity, and following one particularly uneventful week of play I decided to write the roundup as a dialogue between two baseball fans at a tavern.

The next morning Tommy Johnson, one of the bureau's more prosaic souls, came in to man the rewrite desk, examined the previous night's stories, read my roundup, and was horrified. The AP simply didn't do things that way. Forthwith he wrote a revised roundup, merely giving the facts, and had it sent over the wire to the member newspapers.

In those years—the late 1940s—I was much interested in trains and railroads. I was off duty Mondays and Tuesdays, and I came up with the idea of arranging to ride on a Chesapeake and Ohio coal train from Fulton Yards in Richmond down to the coal terminals in Newport News, and write feature stories about that and about the loading of coal aboard ships for export. I asked the bureau chief for permission to do so. He was willing, but so leery was he of running afoul of the Newspaper Guild that he told me to do the writing of the stories while at work.

I made arrangements with the C&O, and on a Monday evening drove over to the yards. When I got back I wrote stories describing the task of getting a long coal train started over the hill just east of the city and the subsequent run through the night to Newport News, and the elaborate operation involved in turning loaded hopper cars upside down and dumping their contents into the holds of ships. The stories were used widely in newspapers within Virginia and in Baltimore. Not a word, however, did the bureau chief have to say about them.

What was I doing, I began to ask myself, sitting in an office five nights a week rewriting other people's stories? I wanted to *write;* that was why I had been drawn to newspaper work. I had thought of joining the Associated Press, becoming an AP staff writer, as a step upward in my career, which would enable me to make wider use of my writing talents. I had expected to have to serve an apprenticeship, but not a total immersion in routine without any prospect of escape from the remorseless requirement of rewriting other people's stories, then rewriting my own rewrites. The thought that if I did my work competently, after several years I might hope to be sent out to cover an occasional story when the state legislature was in session, was scarcely sufficient to keep me satisfied.

That I had made a mistake was obvious. I had let

my youthful notions of what it would mean to be an AP man overwhelm my judgment. Obviously I would have done better to stay in the city editor's job in Staunton and wait for an opportunity to join a large daily newspaper with a staff sufficiently numerous to permit and even encourage different kinds of writing. But I had been too impatient—with the result that I now found myself in a situation from which there was no prospect of extricating myself any time soon.

The question I might have asked myself, however, but did not, was this: Suppose I did find myself a reporter's job on a large newspaper—say the *Richmond Times-Dispatch* or *Baltimore Sun* or *Washington Post.* Would I then be willing to work for some years as a beat reporter, covering routine political or governmental stories or whatever, and writing an occasional feature as the occasion presented itself? Could I honestly say that when a reporter I had *enjoyed* covering the news—that writing about it, no matter how well, satisfied my desire to *write*?

That was the heart of the matter. If I had possessed sufficient self-knowledge and insight into my own emotions, which clearly I did not, I might have realized that right within my own family the identical question had been posed, and not once but in two instances. For there were the contrasting examples of my two uncles. Manning, like all of us on my father's side of the family, had stayed in newspaper work. He had become, successively, city editor and then editorial writer and columnist. When in his twenties and thirties he had also written fiction, publishing stories in various adventure magazines, but had given it up.

Dan had begun as a reporter, worked on newspapers in various cities, and had also written plays, keeping at it until they began getting produced on Broadway. Following several very successful plays in the late 1920s and early 1930s, he had become a screenwriter for Paramount in Hollywood. After not quite a decade of that, between his plays—one had also been a successful movie—and his Hollywood earnings he had saved enough money to live independently, whereupon for the rest of his life he wrote plays, not one of which was ever produced.

Dan told me that what he had learned to do early on was to divide his day into two days. He worked as a reporter, and later a deskman, in the morning and early afternoon, then exercised at the YMCA, after which he went home and took a nap of several hours. When he awoke he went out for dinner, worked at his playwriting through the evening, read for a while, then slept until time to report for work at the newspaper again. He had tremendous willpower—far more, alas, than I did.

Manning was a gentler person, but very taciturn; it

was difficult to converse with him. I asked him once why he had ceased writing fiction, but all he replied was, "I lost interest in it." I also asked Dan why he had left newspaper work. He found, he said, that after a time he grew bored with it. Though considerably more willing to talk about his experiences than Manning, Dan was very much a loner; he lived by himself in a hotel room in western Texas, had no real friends there so far as I knew. Manning lived with my uncle and aunt, and was well known in Charleston, with numerous friends.

Though we shared many interests, neither of them seemed temperamentally very much like me. I did not think that I could live out my life alone, as a bachelor, whether in Charleston or in a hotel room in El Paso.

I did not assume that newspaper work as such was boring, as Dan did; it was only the particular forms of it that I had thus far encountered that had seemed tedious. Writing plays, however, was not where my own literary interests lay. What I liked to read was fiction and history.

Several times I had tried to write novels, but without success; I had never gotten beyond the opening chapters. It seemed to me that what I needed was instruction in how to do it. I assumed that learning how to write fiction was a technical skill which, once acquired, could thereafter be applied at will.

I had heard that there were certain universities which offered graduate instruction not merely in contemporary fiction, but in the writing of it. As a World War II veteran I had been eligible for something like thirty months of college at the government's expense, and had used only seven or eight months of it when finishing up my undergraduate requirements at the University of Richmond. Why not, therefore, apply for admission as a graduate student at a university with a curriculum in creative writing? I could take a year off, learn how to write novels, then return to newspaper work—but not on the AP!—and write fiction on my own.

I looked through college and university catalogs at the Richmond Public Library and identified several such programs. I wrote to the directors of two of them, explaining what I wished to do. The naïveté of my plan, and of my letter describing it, did not occur to me. Paul Engle, at the University of Iowa, wrote back to say that although he was dubious, he would be willing to admit me to that program for one term. Elliott Coleman, at Johns Hopkins, not only agreed to take me, but offered me a fellowship appointment as a junior instructor, whereby I would teach a class in freshman composition and be paid for it. The stipend would double the income I would be receiving from the Veterans Administration.

As a senior in college after the war I had been approached by the chairman of the Romance Languages Department about teaching a class in freshman French during the 1946–1947 school year if I were going to be around. Since I was planning to graduate in August, I had not considered it. I had also thought briefly, not long after being discharged from the Army and resuming school, of going on for graduate study in American history, but the lure of newspaper reporting had been much too powerful. Yet in neither instance had teaching, as such, struck me as a possible vocation. And neither did it do so when I received Elliott Coleman's offer and wrote back to accept it. It was solely a means to an end, a way to earn a little money while learning how to write fiction.

#   #   #

5

INTERLUDE
Baltimore

Except *for a couple of brief episodes on copy desks, to be described in a subsequent sketch, the six years that I spent as a graduate student and teacher of writing at the Johns Hopkins University in Baltimore were not part of my newspaper career, and so are not really germane to this book. Still, something needs to be said about them.*

On the September day when I aimed my eleven-year-old Plymouth coupe northward on U.S. Highway 301 and headed for Baltimore, I was twenty-four years old and still extremely moist behind the ears. As noted, I saw myself as taking a one-year leave from journalism, after which I would return to the profession that since childhood had been my choice for a lifetime's work. I thought of graduate study as a kind of literary trade school, offering vocational training. I knew that I could write decent English prose, and I liked to read novels, so I assumed that once I had been taught how to manage certain mechanical problems involving plot and characterization, I would be able to produce publishable fiction—in much the same way that a baker combines yeast, flour, salt, sugar, butter, and water in the proper proportions to make Parker House rolls.

Now in point of fact there were certain academic operations that approached the art of fiction in just such formulaic fashion, but what their students were taught to write was popular magazine fiction for the pulps and slicks—the terms referring to the kind of paper that magazines were printed on. The pulps used coarse woodpulp and offered highly plotted adventure, detective, western, and other crude fictional entertainment, and the slicks provided popular fiction of a more sophisticated nature, likewise formulaic but with relatively more complication in the characters. The fiction that I read and wanted to learn how to write, however, was not aimed at mass magazine audiences. It was literary fiction, which was the kind that was studied and taught at the Department of Writing, Speech, and Drama—after 1953 the Writing Seminars—at the Johns Hopkins University.

Only it wasn't taught! For what I discovered upon arrival was that there were lecture courses offered in James Joyce, Marcel Proust, and the history of literary criticism, but no classes in the writing of fiction. The only "creative writ-

*ing" as such being offered was poetry, taught by Karl
Shapiro, who had recently won the Pulitzer Prize and was
one of the best-known of the younger contemporary poets.*

*Thus the instruction in how to write novels that I had
left newspaper work to receive wasn't even available at Johns
Hopkins that year. Yet I had not been there for two weeks before I knew that I had made no mistake in coming, and
whether or not I ever learned how to write publishable fiction
became of less immediate concern to me than the kind of literary study I was now doing.*

*For the first time in my life I was with a group of peo-
ple, faculty and fellow graduate students alike, for whom it
was more important to write well than for a large audience,
and whose notion of what constituted good writing centered
on its capacity for emotional complexity. The writing they admired, their approach to what writing was all about, their assumption that there was room for nothing short of the utmost
intelligence in reading and writing fiction and poetry, their
willingness to confront the full range of their feelings in what
they wrote, were a revelation to me.*

*That most of the fellow apprentices with whom I was
now associated were able to attain those goals only very approximately indeed, and that the ratio of light to heat in our
common efforts was not very favorable, was not important.
Neither was the fact that in what all of us were engaged in
doing, the potentiality for humbuggery and deception, very
much including self-deception, was always present. Certainly*

it was not always possible at first to distinguish what was difficult to understand because it dealt with difficult, complex material from what was difficult because it trafficked in superficially clever fashion with vague ideas and counterfeit emotions. But that did not finally matter, for whatever the transient allure of the spurious, the genuine and honest was bound to emerge, and when it did it was unmistakable.

This was the kind of writing that counted, and I could see now that it was the kind that I wanted to do. But I had so much to learn, and also so much to unlearn—easy evasions, lazy ways to secure gaudy effects, false fronts and facades. The best newspaper writing, like the best writing of any kind, possessed lucidity and muscularity, and was fresh and clear in the honesty of its telling. But it had been deceptively easy to settle for what was immediate and facile, and writing as I had been doing for an uncritical audience for so many years, I had picked up tricks, contrivances, and dodges that, now that I was attempting to examine and to recreate some of the complication of what I thought and felt, kept getting in my way, leading me along alluring but false paths, and instead of clarifying my vision blurring it.

And of course, being by nature hard-headed and resistant mentally to whatever was not immediately evident, I fought against my own perceptions every step of the way and attempted to deny what, in spite of myself, I was absorbing. As a writer my middle-class attitudes and ways of seeing things could become a source of considerable strength, and help to protect me from preciosity and pedantry, but only if they were kept from coarsening and desensitizing my capacity for thinking and feeling. I needed to learn to read with greater care than I had been accustomed to expend, and not to become impatient with whatever seemed difficult, since in no other way would I ever, as a reader, come to understand my own emotional experience and make it available to me as a writer.

In short, if literature and the literary imagination were important enough to me to make me wish to let them be a central part of my life, then I had one hell of a lot to learn.

That, most of all, is what I realized during my first year of absence from the newspaper writing that I still assumed was to be my vocation, and it was why, when the end of the second term began to draw closer, I was reluctant to leave Johns Hopkins.

Please understand that it was not that I thought it all out in abstract terms like that. What I did know was that I was now doing something that interested me more than anything else I had ever tried, and that I had scarcely even begun to explore its potentialities.

The truth was that I was incredibly lucky. What it was that Elliott Coleman, the chairman of Writing, Speech, and Drama, saw that led him to believe that a naïve young newspaperman, reasonably well read in literature in general but woefully ignorant of almost all the best writing done in the twentieth century, might some day be capable of a profes-

sional career in modern letters, is more than I can imagine. Yet somehow he thought so. He not only kept me on as a teacher, but gave me the department's nondescript literary quarterly to resurrect and edit, assigned me to teach a graduate workshop in the writing of fiction when as yet I had published no literary fiction whatever of my own, and encouraged my interest in modern southern literature.

Within four years the literary quarterly, the Hopkins Review, *without ever being able to pay one cent to its contributors, was nationally known and distributed, its fiction was several times chosen for republication in the* Best American Short Stories *volumes, it introduced to American readers the work of leading Continental literary theorists such as Erich Auerbach, Georges Poulet, Ernst Robert Curtius, and Leo Spitzer, and it began publishing the symposium in modern southern literature that has since been credited with establishing the subject as a field of critical scholarship.*

All this was done not only without the help of, but often in the face of the active hostility of, the University's English Department, which held as a pedagogical principle that no literature written after the year 1900 or by any still-living author whatsoever was an appropriate topic for graduate literary inquiry. The result was that as Elliott Coleman's Department of Writing, Speech, and Drama prospered and its graduates began publishing books, so did the intensity and vehemence of the English Department's opposition. Even though almost all the internationally distinguished, mainly

European scholars in philosophy, romance languages, and German on the University faculty were partisans of Elliott's program, it was the professors of the English Department who had the ear of the Johns Hopkins administration.

In 1952–1953 the shootout came. Elliott was no politician, while his opponents were academic politicos of the first order. The result was that the operations of Elliott's department were severely cut back and renamed the Writing Seminars, his staff was thereafter limited to a single instructor with a three-years-maximum, nonrenewable appointment, and the burgeoning Hopkins Review *was denied the pitifully small increase in funds needed to keep it alive, and so folded. As for myself, I was given one more, terminal year as an instructor, and that was that.*

By then I was married, with my wife at work on a doctorate in political science. I did not have a doctorate, for I would not submit myself to the massive pedantry of the English Department Ph.D. program. Yet I was determined to continue writing about and studying modern southern literature, and to make my way with an M.A. degree alone.

No teaching jobs in literature beckoned, but I was offered an assistant professorship in the School of Journalism of the University of Missouri, teaching feature writing with the possibility of a tie-in with the English Department there, and I was about to accept.

Then came word that the Sewanee Review, *a literary quarterly, had received funds from the Rockefeller Founda-*

*tion to award three one-year fellowships, each with a stipend
of $3,000, and that thanks to Allen Tate and others I was
in line to be awarded one of them. The Johns Hopkins hu-
manities division was developing an interdepartmental doctoral program in the study of aesthetics and literary theory.
Its director, the philosopher George Boas, together with Elliott, urged me to stay on for one more school year and earn a
doctorate in it. In effect I had been working with the practice
and the history of literary criticism for the past several years,
Boas pointed out. I need take no courses, but only pass an
examination on the history of literary theory and criticism. I
had also written the first draft of a book on Thomas Wolfe,
time, and the South, which I was planning to rewrite; I could
use that as a dissertation, Boas said, with the French phe-
nomenological critic Georges Poulet as director.*

*So I stayed on for my terminal year as an instructor,
rewrote the book as a dissertation, received a contract for its
publication, studied for and passed the examination in literary criticism, delivered a paper on Thomas Wolfe at the Modern Language Association meetings, defended my dissertation
before a committee of fifteen professors, and received the doctorate. Meanwhile the symposium in contemporary southern
literature,* Southern Renascence: The Literature of the
Modern South, *was published as a book and reviewed.*

*Thus ended my time at Johns Hopkins. The one-year
hiatus in my career as newspaperman had become a six-year
interlude. I was now an accredited scholar, with a Ph.D. for*

union card—but with no prospect for a teaching position in sight, for I still didn't really Belong to the Lodge. I had, after all, in effect thumbed my nose at the pedants at Johns Hopkins who controlled the field of American literature there, which was where my dissertation and my interests lay. Without accredited sponsors in the field in which I had written my dissertation and wanted to teach, even the backing of scholars such as Boas, Poulet, and the historian C. Vann Woodward was of insufficient influence in that time of few academic teaching vacancies.

There was one kind of daily journalism that I had not done, except briefly once as a fill-in: editorial writing. Writing editorials might be a way of bridging my two interests, in that I would not be doing factual news reporting but writing pieces of analysis and interpretation. I felt sure, too, that with what I had now learned—and what I had begun to understand about myself—I would also be able to continue to write literary criticism, and perhaps even the novel that I still wanted to write.

I corresponded with a newspaper in St. Petersburg, Florida, about writing editorials, and was invited to come down for a look. Another newspaper out in the Pacific Northwest offered me a position in which I would work exclusively at writing feature articles, especially on the outdoors, with occasional editorials if I wished. If I were to return to journalism, either sounded tempting.

Before I could make up my mind to travel down to Florida and talk with the people there, however, Fate, or Fortune, or Luck, or whatever it was, again intervened. George Boas was a member of the executive council of the American Studies Association, a learned society of academics interested in various phases of American culture. The association had received a developmental grant from the Carnegie Corporation, and was in search of an executive secretary to set up headquarters at the University of Pennsylvania and work with the society's various regional groups. Boas nominated me.

I went down to Washington, where a search committee was interviewing candidates for the secretaryship. When the interview was over I felt that it had gone poorly and there was no chance of my being chosen. To my surprise, however, two days later I was offered the position, which carried with it an assistant professorship of American civilization at the University of Pennsylvania. Later I learned that each of the three members of the search committee had his own candidate, and I was everybody's second choice. So I got the job. At the end of June 1954, I bade goodbye to the Johns Hopkins University, and we headed for Philadelphia. So ended my Baltimore interlude.

But meanwhile I have gotten well ahead of the story of my apprenticeship in newspapers and newspaper work. So in what follows it will be necessary to go back six years to the time when, having had a bellyful of rewriting my own rewrites for the Richmond bureau of the Associated Press, I left my chosen profession and enrolled in graduate school. My next lesson in journalism as a would-be vocation would be as a copy editor.

\# \# \#

6

REMEMBRANCE OF COPY DESKS PAST

Back several decades before desktop computers came along, when Truman and Eisenhower were consuls and I was young and habitually in need of cash, on daily newspapers of medium-to-metropolitan size there was an institution known as the copy desk, manned by persons known as copy editors. Theirs was a skilled trade, like bartending or bricklaying. By the salary standards of newspapers—which were not very lofty salary standards then—it paid reasonably well. For that reason, though temperamentally unsuited for it, on occasion I practiced the craft.

As careers in journalism went it was something of a dead-end operation, which is to say, the instances of a copy editor being promoted to a higher calling on the staff of a paper were rare. The most he—and all the copy editors that I ever knew were males—might aspire to was to become chief of the copy desk upon the retirement or demise of the current occupant of the slot, and even then the chances were that someone else in the newsroom hierarchy not then associated with the copy desk would be assigned to direct its activities.

Copy editors tended to be middle-aged or elderly, possessed of education and occasionally even erudition, of sedentary habits and, if not always placid, then quiescent disposition. To say that what they did for a living was of a highly routine nature would be an understatement. Their presence in a newsroom was, how shall I say, reflexive—taken for granted, assumed, and totally without luminosity or *éclat*. A copy editor's role was something like that of professional baseball umpires: necessary to the game, but performed best when attracting no notice whatever.

They were drawn to their occupation, or more accurately, happened upon it not through design or ambition but from a mixture of aptitude and disposition. Almost no young man ever began in journalism as a copy editor; in one way or another all had originally set out to be reporters. But by no means all persons who were hired to be reporters subsequently demonstrated a flair for gathering the news. The virtues of not a few reporters turned out to consist of stolidity and a capacity for writing down details. It was from the ranks of these that copy editors were generally recruited.

Usually it happened as follows. After such a reporter had been handling prescribed assignments for some few years, it became incumbent upon the management to pay him a higher salary. So the reporter was moved up to a desk job such as assistant state editor, assistant city editor, or assistant something. Years might then go by, until a new managing editor or city editor set out to shake up the established order and get some more direction and excitement into his paper's coverage of news. Or perhaps a veteran copy editor reached retirement age. Or maybe both.

Whereat the long-ago-reporter-turned-assistant-telegraph-editor or whatever was transferred to the copy desk, and there he worked away, editing stories, writing headlines, checking proof, providing routine competence where routine competence was what was needed. As for whether he positively enjoyed the work, or merely found it a tolerable form of employment, I will say only that, for the kind of newspaperman I am attempting to describe, the distinction between the two might not ordinarily have occurred to him.

There were other routes by which people arrived at the copy desk. They might have been onetime sports or entertainment columnists who had grown overly chummy with promoters, or city editors turned too curmudgeonish for maintaining an acceptable level of staff morale, or aging beat reporters adjudged to have lost their zeal for cultivating news sources. Or it might be that someone who had not been a newspaperman at all but possessed the required erudition and quiescence was in need of a job, and through some connection or the other found employment on a copy desk; this last route was uncommon but not unknown. And of course there was the born copy editor, the individual who temperamentally, vocationally, and by aptitude actively preferred the kind of labor that the copy desk required to all other forms of journalistic employment. I don't know that I ever encountered such a person, but I assume that they existed.

If I seem to be conveying the impression that newspaper copy desks were staffed primarily by those who were putting in time, it was, so far as I could ever tell, true; I don't believe that I ever met one who wasn't. I was told that on certain large metropolitan newspapers, notably the *New York Times,* being a copy editor meant something more than checking news stories for grammatical and stylistic errors and writing headlines for those stories, and that copy editors on such papers were also expected to verify all the factual statements and to evaluate the soundness of what the reporters were asserting. On such papers, it was said, during the course of an entire day's work a copy editor might work on no more than one or two stories, and if more than one then on closely related topics; and that he was expected to be more than ordinarily well informed about the subject of the story.

If so, certainly this was not how the copy desk functioned on any paper I ever encountered. For one thing, given the number of stories to be edited and headlined in each issue of the paper and the number of copy editors available to handle them, there would not have been nearly time enough for that kind of editing. For another, none of the middle-aged and elderly gentlemen alongside whom I worked as copy editor ever showed signs that I can recall of being practicing authorities in particular areas of knowledge, whether local, state, or national government, foreign policy, the professions, the arts, crime and punishment, geographical locales, or whatever. They were simply not the type. As shall shortly be seen, I did work with one who was a university teacher of philosophy with a doctorate in his field; but what he was an authority on was the parimutuel boards at Pimlico, Laurel, and Bowie.

Most copy desks shared certain traits. I never saw one that was importantly blessed with humor, though I am told that there were some that were. Newsrooms were frequently the scenes of much hilarity; a great deal of bantering and teasing customarily went on, even in those ruled over by stuffed shirts—as some were, for there was a type of news executive to whom the role of Mogul came naturally. (I recall one who was caught hunting ducks over baited fields in violation of the game laws. When he returned to his office after his appearance in court, it was to find his desk heaped high with kernels of corn.) On any newspaper for which I ever worked, even including the *Baltimore Sun,* the reporters were doing funny things. But the tide of mirth customarily rolled only up to the edge of the copy desk, where it halted and rose no further.

I am not sure why this was so, but I suspect that it had something to do with the fact that copy editors were, as a species, staid creatures. No doubt there were exceptions, but I recall none. They worked at their stories and headlines; when there were none to do, most of them read the paper or did crossword puzzles. There was relatively little conversation of any kind. If a group of reporters occupied places next to each other in the newsroom, there was almost always a great deal of bantering back and forth going on. Not so on the copy desk; conversation was customarily at a minimum. When I first worked on a copy desk I thought, being in my mid-twenties when everyone else was middle-aged or older, that it was the difference in age that made it so difficult to hold a conversation, but then I began to realize that neither did the others do much conversing among themselves. This was true even of people who had worked side by side for years. There was something about the copy desk that made for gravity, or else something about the kind of work that copy editors did that caused the sober-minded to find a home there.

Desk jobs are by definition sedentary, but most city or state or telegraph editors moved about the news-room from time to time. Not so copy editors; a job on the copy desk was certainly not for anyone who liked to be on the prowl. The only walking that was done involved occasional trips over to the unabridged dic-tionary stand to check definitions and spellings. I am told that an occupational disease, from sitting at a copy desk so regularly and for so long at a time, was hemor-rhoids, and I do not doubt it; I noticed that most copy editors made a point of bringing cushions to work.

They were—or the ones I knew were—careful, precise, often finickal creatures. All had little habits, mannerisms, idiosyncrasies. One might like to keep his copy pencils arranged in a symmetrical row on the desk; upon selecting one to work with, he took care to align all the others by size, like organ pipes, before getting to work on the copy. Another might decline to use the office pencil sharpener, and whenever not at work on copy busy himself keeping individual points on his pencils with a penknife. Another might bring along little slips of colored paper for writing trial headlines on before inscribing the completed version onto the standard half-sheet of copy paper. Another kept a small tin box on his desk, and each night, upon arriving at work, emptied the contents of a package of Smith Bros. cough drops into it, afterward consuming one after the other throughout the evening. As preventative medicine they must have been effective, for I never once heard him cough.

Newspaper copy editors had two basic functions. They edited copy—i.e., checked news and feature stories for factual accuracy, conformity to style, and grammatical correctness—and they wrote headlines. The latter was the more demanding task. Their activities were presided over by a copy desk chief, installed inside a U-shaped desk from which he handed out the stories to be edited and headlined to the copy editors seated about him on the outside of the desk. The space inside the U was known as the slot, and the outside as the rim.

There were certain kinds of news that a copy desk did not ordinarily handle. On some papers the wire service copy from the Associated Press was handled by a separate telegraph desk. The sports department did its own copy editing, and on large metropolitan papers had its own smaller but full-fledged copy desk. The editorials and related items—letters to the editor, syndicated columns, matters involving the expression of opinion in general—were always handled separately. In my day the society pages—weddings, engagements, social events—were likewise not entrusted to the copy desk, in part because it was crucial to be aware of which families counted and which didn't. Most papers of any size had a resident *arbiter elegantiarum* who knew at once that this young lady was of debutante status and bound for the Junior League after marriage, while that one, no matter that her father could buy and sell large chunks of the downtown city, was not. Thus the former's doings rated a prominent place on the first society page, while the latter's were to receive lesser notice. Indeed, on metropolitan papers such as the *New York Herald-Tribune* of sainted memory, only the social arrangements of the upper-level gentry achieved publication at all.

But that is another story, and without relevance for the essentially plebeian activities of the copy desk. Since the skills cultivated by copy editors back in the days of hot type are in danger of receding into the darkness of time along with those of the iceman, the wainwright, and the village blacksmith, I propose for the sake of posterity to make an effort to sketch them here.

The professional tools of a copy editor consisted of pencils, paper, a wire basket, and, to one side, on a table next to his place on the rim, a typewriter. If new to the job he kept a style book and headline schedule close by. The pencils were of soft lead and without erasers. Depending upon whether the budgetary prac-

tices of the newspaper's business manager were gener-
ous or miserly, they might be in abundant or scarce
supply; I have known newspapers whose managing
editor doled out copy pencils one or two at a time,
like wafers at a communion service, the meanwhile
that the publisher traveled to and from his office in a
chauffeur-driven Cadillac Fleetwood. The paper was
copy paper—newsprint, including a supply of 8½-by-
11 sheets cut in half to be used for writing headlines.

The typewriter was always a standard model, usually an Underwood, Remington, or L. C. Smith; for
reasons unknown to me few newsrooms were
equipped with Royals. The age of the typewriter was
likely to be venerable; when I labored on copy desks I
was in my middle to late twenties, and I doubt that I
was ever assigned a typewriter that was not older than
myself. During my several years on newspapers I never
once witnessed a new typewriter being installed in a
newsroom. I suppose the secretaries and clerks in the
business office got the new ones, on the theory that
the correspondence and documents they wrote might
be read by someone important, while the news staff's
output need be read only by the printers in the composing room. In any event, when in the 1970s newspapers began changing over to electronic keyboards
and phototypesetting, there must have been some no-
table bargains in antique office machinery available to
collectors.

Each newspaper had its own typographical style and design, and the various headlines used were drawn from compatible typefaces. Thus one newspaper—typically though not always a morning paper—might draw upon a series of headlines in serifed type, say Cheltenham with some Garamond for variety, while another, usually an afternoon paper, would feature sans serif faces such as Franklin Gothic. Within each such headline family were alternatives having to do with type style, whether bold or lite (never light), Roman or italic, condensed or extended, unadorned or with a ruled border or box all or part-way around the headline. A headline could be spread over eight columns, in which case it was known as a streamer, but most were designed for single-column display.

The size of the type—14 or 18 point for three- and four-paragraph items meriting only little two-line heads, and from there on up to 84 point for page-wide streamers—and the number of lines in the headline depended upon the placement on the page. In addition to the main headline itself, and depending upon the importance of the story and its positioning on the page, a headline could also contain one or more tiers, or banks, of smaller type.

From this multiplicity of potential combinations, the newspaper's designers evolved a finite series of headline displays, which were designated by letter or number or both. A sample set was displayed for a headline schedule, and from these the design of each day's front and inside pages was worked out. The page layout was determined not by the copy desk but by higher-ups, in accordance with what would be available in the way of news that day and how important such stories might be.

The stories to be edited would be turned over to the chief of the copy desk, who would then select a copy editor to edit each story and prepare its headline. A wire story, unlike one written locally, required very little editing. It was generally considered taboo to re-work the language of a story bearing the AP logotype, though several stories might be rewritten into a single account which was then preceded by the credit "From wire reports." Otherwise the only editing done was to underline the necessary capitalization, for teletype copy arrived in all-capital letters, and to make the style conform to the local paper's practice.

The quantity and importance of wire service news was such that the majority of newspapers had adapted their own stylistics to the AP's. There were, however, holdouts, such as the *Baltimore Sun,* which had their own way of doing things. Given the temperament of copy desk chiefs—the majority of whom, I suspect, had been toilet trained too early by their mothers—it was woe unto any copy editor who failed to change, for example, "25th Ave. N.W." to "Twenty-Fifth Ave. NW" if that was the local paper's style, or neglected to capitalize East when it referred to a section of the city rather than a direction, and so on. On such occasions I have seen gaskets blown by choleric desk chiefs.

The copy having been edited, it was time to write the headline. In the era when I labored on copy desks, most newspapers were in the process of emancipating themselves from the earlier practice of carefully balanced page makeup—headlines of equal size on corresponding halves of the front page, with the headline type elaborately staggered and indented. It had dawned on the authorities that from the standpoint of the reader glancing over the headlines on the front page to see what was doing in the world that day, it really did not make a great deal of difference whether the headline type was all flush left—i.e., set evenly along the left margin of the column—or placed in tiers, each line indented one em underneath the preceding line, an em being the width of a lower-case "m" in that size of type. In earlier years, however, no such laxity was permitted on most newspapers with pretensions to professional rectitude, which resulted in much effort being expended in efforts to condense the main points of news stories in intricate combinations of display type.

Consider, for example, the verbal ingenuity required to produce the following headline, with its two banks, which appeared on the front page of the *Norfolk Virginian-Pilot* for June 13, 1917:

PROGRESS OF LIBERTY LOAN SINCE FRIDAY GRATIFYING

—

Treasury Officials, However, Unable To Estimate Total Subscription Owing To Failure Of Banks To Report —Urgent Call Goes Out

—

BIG EFFORT NECESSARY; AN APPEAL ISSUED

Headlines on some papers were even more elaborately spaced than that; and in any case a fastidious copy desk chief—and many were—might have insisted that a preposition should not be used at the end of the top line, that there was much too much white space between the words of the third line of the first bank, and that the two lines of the second bank ought to be more nearly equal in length. As must be evident, considerable dexterity was required to write a headline to such specifications.

By midcentury many newspapers had dropped such intricate headline typography, but even the relative freedom of flush-left heads could still entail considerable skill—and certainly the onset of phototypesetting by computer has not importantly altered the fact that the larger the size of type being used, the fewer the characters that can be fitted into the width of a column. One need only contemplate the difficulties that a copy editor at work in the year 1991, by which time hot type was gone from the scene, would face in writing a single-column, all-capital-letters headline, in say 24-point type, for a news story about the Gulf War that centered upon a pronouncement by General Norman Schwarzkopf. Unlike an earlier and more prominent general and later president who could be designated as Ike, no such single-syllable alternative existed. A tabloid such as the *New York Daily News* might be breezy enough in its ways to permit the general to be denoted as "NORM"—as for example:

NO LET-UP
IN AIR WAR,
NORM SAYS

But what if the copy editor was working for a newspaper such as all those that I ever wrote for, in whose headlines no such slangy familiarity would be

countenanced? It would then be up to the copy editor
to figure out another way to say what was needed,
such as

NO LET-UP
SAID LIKELY
FOR AIR WAR

or perhaps

IRAQ SKIES
WILL STAY
TARGETED

The name of the person issuing the pronouncement
would have to be identified only in the bank:

Bombing to Continue,
Schwarzkopf Warns

which would make the assertion seem less personal-
ized.

In general, except for their headlines the local news
stories required more attention than those from the
wire service, because although it was not necessary to
go through them and underline the capital letters, a
staff reporter's grammar, spelling, and syntax were con-

sidered eligible for corrective grammatical action, and peculiarities of local usage were more apt to figure in the account. Theoretically the city desk was supposed to have caught any violations of local reference before passing the story on to the copy desk, but when copy descended upon news desks in quantity, mistakes could slip by. It was therefore important for a copy editor to know that a prominent local businessman spelled his name Rhoads, not Rhodes, that a downtown thoroughfare was spelled Greene rather than Green Street no matter how the police blotter had it recorded, that a locally prominent family spelled its name Steuart and not Stuart or Stewart, and so on. A veteran copy editor was often a compendium of such knowledge; he might not be able to write three consecutive sentences without setting a faithful reader to nodding, but he knew that Ellicott's Mills took an apostrophe but Sparrows Point did not.

As for my own brief and irregular career as a copy editor, it was certainly never my intention to prepare myself for such work. It was rather that I acquired the technical skills that were involved in copy editing while engaged in various other journalistic activities, including editing high school and college newspapers, working as a reporter on a small weekly, editing a newspaper in the Army during World War II, and after graduation from college working as a reporter and then as city editor. The last, as noted earlier, was on a very small daily newspaper, for which I selected and edited both the local and telegraph copy, diagrammed the pages, wrote the headlines, then supervised the making up of the pages in the composing room. In short, by the time I was in my early twenties I had learned how to do just about everything that was done on a copy desk.

As also remarked previously, during my planned temporary respite from journalism at the Johns Hopkins University's Writing Seminars, as they are now titled, I found that I greatly enjoyed being involved in literary study and teaching English. Yet at the same time, there were aspects of newspaper work that I missed, in particular the company of other newsmen. At Johns Hopkins two of my fellow graduate students, Russell Baker and Bill Gresham, were working nights as beginning reporters on the *Baltimore Sun,* and some evenings, after working on my writing in my room until midnight, I would drive over to the East Baltimore Police Station Precinct, where they were manning the press room, sit around them with until they were free for the evening, and go out for beer and a sandwich.

Even so, as the school year drew to an end I was reluctant to leave Johns Hopkins. I decided to look for a newspaper position within driving distance of Baltimore, so that I could teach an adult-education class in English composition one night a week and continue to be part of the Writing Seminars community. So little insight did I have into my own personality and capabilities that what I went looking for was a position that would be as routine as possible, involving a minimum of writing. My theory was that with a job that I could put out of my mind when the workday was over, I would preserve my energies to concentrate on the writing that I intended to do. My recent experience with handling a totally routine job with the Associated Press did not deter me in the slightest.

I wrote letters to an assortment of newspapers, and when the *Wilmington Morning News* in Delaware offered me a job on its copy desk, I accepted it at once. Wilmington was no more than sixty miles from Baltimore, I would be working five nights a week, with Sundays and Mondays off, and the $60-a-week salary was considerably more than I had been getting by on for the past nine months. Not only that, but the stipend for the adult-education class I would be teaching on Monday evenings at Johns Hopkins would cover the cost of hotel and meals in Baltimore.

Thus at age twenty-five I became a copy editor. Five nights a week, from 4 P.M. until the first copies of the

Morning News came off the press and were delivered to the copy desk for checking sometime after midnight, I worked on the rim. Each evening I was handed a succession of stories, mostly local pieces of a lesser nature until I learned the lay of the land, to be edited and given headlines, usually of the two-line variety. It did not take long to learn the newspaper's headline varieties and styles.

I lived in a rented room approximately a mile from downtown Wilmington. Even though my job on the Associated Press in Richmond had been deadly dull, I had enjoyed the companionship of some of the people I worked with, persons my own age with whom I played golf and shared some interests. Not so in Wilmington. There was no one on the paper's reportorial staff whose interests, so far as I ever knew, converged in the slightest with mine. Most were older persons, settled residents of Delaware and married, with families. During all the time I was there I do not recall ever going out to eat dinner at a restaurant with anyone on the staff.

As for the copy desk, in addition to the slot man there were three other habitués. The slot man himself was also telegraph editor, and he kept busy throughout the evening. The man on my left, who was in his forties, was interested in one thing only: horseracing. When not at work editing copy or writing headlines he read the *Daily Racing Form* and the racing pages in the Philadelphia papers. On one occasion he invited me to go out to Delaware Park with him—in my car. I had never been to a racetrack before and was curious to see what it was all about. During the course of the afternoon he borrowed money from me to make several bets. The horses he backed all lost, and the loan was never repaid. The next day the city editor, the one member of the news staff with whom I was congenial, remarked that he should have warned me against going to the races with the man, and under no circumstances to lend him any money for betting.

On my right at the copy desk was a round-faced, middle-aged man with large lips, who came over from Philadelphia each evening. He smoked cigars incessantly, or rather, chewed on them, occasionally touching a match to one and puffing for a few moments before letting it go out again. In this way he could make a single cigar last for an hour or more, discarding it only after it had become so abbreviated in length that when time came to relight he looked to be in peril of burning his nose. When not at work it was his custom to remove from his desk drawer a supply of kraft envelopes he kept there, containing photographs of scantily clad females clipped from *Film Fun* and other educational publications. He would shuffle through the contents of an envelope, appraising each photo in turn while meanwhile moving the cigar about with his lips. If time then permitted, he would begin on another envelope.

The third copy editor was a gardener who spent his unoccupied time at the desk thumbing through seed manuals. In midsummer, as his gardening fructified, he sometimes bought a supply of tomatoes, squash, cucumbers, and the like to work, for distribution among the news staff members. Having no access to kitchen or icebox and taking all my meals in restaurants, I had no occasion to avail myself of his bounty. If he had any interests other than gardening I never found them out.

In all, I did not find my colleagues on the *Morning News* an inspiring lot, and have no doubt that from their standpoint I constituted no enthralling addition to the staff, either. The one exception was the city editor, W. Emerson Wilson, who turned out to be a Confederate buff, an amateur painter, and considerable of a reader. After I left we kept in touch over the years, until his death in 1982. Other than Wilson I made no friends on the newspaper staff, and he was fifteen years older than myself, married and with children.

What I found was what I should have anticipated but did not, which was that the notion that I could spend eight hours each evening doing dull, routine desk work, then work on my own writing during the day, was totally unrealistic. Whatever might be true for others, I was incapable of separating what I did for a living from what interested me; nor was I equipped emotionally to live and write in a social vacuum. On Sundays I could drive down to Baltimore, but it was summer and most of my friends at the university, male and female, were out of town.

By midsummer I realized that it was not going to work. The chairman of the Writing Seminars at Johns Hopkins offered to find me an additional class to teach, and I still had some eligibility left on my educational benefits from my Army service. I could pick up a little extra money writing newspaper feature stories. So I gave notice and moved back to Baltimore, where however straitened my finances, I would be doing work that I wanted to do. Thus ended my first stint on a newspaper copy desk.

A little more than a year later, in the fall of 1950, I was a full-time instructor in the Writing Seminars, with a twelve-month salary, but one so low that I was getting into debt. Moreover, I was planning to be married the following spring, and I needed to save up some money. So I wrote to the *Baltimore Sun* to ask whether it had need of a part-time copy editor. In reply I was invited to come in for an interview. I was given a piece of telegraph copy and asked to edit it and write a headline, and when done was offered a job working Friday, Saturday, and Sunday evenings on the copy desk, at $75 a week, which was more than my salary as an instructor.

This time I was under no illusions; I knew the copy-editing routine would be tedious. But I needed money, and I would have to trade weekend evenings for it until either my teaching salary improved or I completed and sold a novel, or else my wife-to-be, who was a graduate student in political science, could also begin earning some money.

The *Baltimore Sun* was a much larger paper than the *Wilmington Morning News,* with various editions. There were half-a-dozen men on the rim in addition to the slot man. I knew several of the reporters, including Russell Baker. I reported for duty at 6 P.M. each evening and worked until after 1 A.M.

I was curious to see how the *Sun*'s copy-desk personnel would stack up in comparison with what I had encountered in Wilmington. They turned out to be, all things considered, somewhat more animated, but essentially they were the same kind of rather shopworn veterans as those I had worked with earlier, and indeed most of the regulars on any copy desk of any newspaper I have ever encountered anywhere.

Only a few of those I worked alongside register in my memory. There was a middle-aged Irishman, his cheeks and jowls purplish from the off-duty consumption of alcohol, who had political opinions about everything, which he aired in a heavy East Baltimore—pronounced Ball-a-mer—accent. There was a permanent assistant professor of philosophy, the sort who, having completed his doctorate and received academic tenure some years back, thereafter taught introductory classes while holding down a second job in order to earn money to bet on horses, for while his mind was in philosophy his heart was at the two-dollar window. What I remember about him is that when editing copy and writing headlines he liked to work with pencils that had been sharpened until they had been worn down to no more than two to three inches in length. He kept a dozen or more of these on his desk, and since the stage at which he found a pencil usable was that at which for most copy editors it became unusable, he was always assured of an adequate supply. I have the impression that as copy editors went, he was considered a good one.

There were other regulars on the copy desk, and I remember them as being generally competent at their trade, but none of them sticks in my mind. What does very much remain vivid in my memory is the personality of the chief of the desk, a man named Bob Murray. Russ Baker, having observed the copy desk at work from across the newsroom for several years, used to talk approvingly of Murray. "He has a set of dogs and bums and drunks working for him, and he whips them through their paces, and gets the paper out every morning," he would say in admiration. I felt much less kindly disposed to the man.

There were various stories about Murray. One was that he had been a police reporter in Norfolk who had been known for having extremely close ties with the cops—so much so that in effect he was considered to be their spokesman. This, I later found out, was true. Another was that he had been a graduate student, had written his doctoral dissertation, and was seated in a hotel room checking it. The manuscript was lying on a table next to an open window, and a sudden gust of wind blew most of it out of into the street below, whereupon he abandoned plans for a career in scholarship and became a journalist. Whether this was true I never learned, but it sounds improbable.

What I do know is that he was a man in his fifties or sixties, and greatly overweight, with what hair remained to him slicked back over his pate after the manner of William Jennings Bryan. He was a type that I observed sometimes in newsrooms: the autocrat whose ego flourishes on the role of hard-boiled chief. There were several such on the staff of the *Baltimore Sun,* taking their cue from the managing editor, a red-faced man named Dorsey and known as Buck, who strode about the newsroom like Erich von Stroheim in *pickelhaube* playing a German general on the Western Front, glancing neither to left nor right and without even a nod of recognition for anyone. I had nothing to do with him and was glad I didn't, having had my fill of such characters in the Army.

With Bob Murray, however, I could not avoid contact, for it was he who handed out the stories to be edited and who inspected the headlines written for them. I had the sense that he had been kicked upstairs to his present position. In any event, for my first several nights on the desk he was polite, and showed me the various kinds of headlines used by the *Sun*. Then abruptly his manner changed and he turned mean. I decided that I was expected to undergo some kind of initiation process, and I determined not to let it anger me.

After a couple of months of working weekends on the copy desk I felt less of a sense of being On Trial. However, I found that I did not much care for the atmosphere of the newsroom. The *Sun,* and its afternoon counterpart the *Evening Sun,* were very good newspapers; of that there was no doubt. They maintained bureaus in overseas capitals, had their own Washington staff, and certain of their newsmen were nationally known for the authority with which they wrote about politics. Yet an aura of provincialism lay over all, an element of self-conscious smugness, of pretending to be not just a well-written, well-edited daily newspaper, but one that was Unique In The Annals Of Journalism. To be selected to work on the *Sun,* in whatever capacity, was held to be a certification of journalistic distinction. Along with the self-satisfaction went an attitude that any and all nonjournalists, mere citizens of the Republic such as politicians, businessmen, professional men, educators, and so forth, were inferior, self-serving creatures, to be viewed sardonically. The patronizing mode pervaded everything.

For all that, I think I would have remained longer on the copy desk of the *Sun* if it had not been for the quite unnecessary atmosphere of unpleasantness generated by Murray. During all the time that I was there I do not recall him even once engaging in casual conversation with any of the copy editors, most of whom were twice my age or more and had been working at the paper for years. It was as if a sizable slab of ice had been installed at the center of the desk, so that all nearby felt the chill.

On one occasion, upon handing me a story to be edited, he remarked, "All right, Mister College Professor, if you're so smart let's see if you can put a headline on this." In retrospect, for all I know it might even have been meant as affability, in however twisted a way, but that was not the tone in which it was said, and it was certainly not how I took it. "You've got the right to criticize my work," I answered, "but don't go making any personal remarks like that."

He made no reply, and went back to his work. I glanced around at the copy desk. Everyone was working away, eyes intent upon what they were doing, as if they had heard nothing. I edited the story, wrote the headline, turned them in, and no more was said.

A couple of months later it was getting along into the spring, and I decided that I had had enough of three nights of copy editing per week done in the ambiance of a police station. I had been able to pay off my bills and even put a little money aside, and would be getting married in June. I was writing a weekly book column for the *Richmond News-Leader,* and while it did not pay nearly as well as what I was earning from the *Baltimore Sun,* between that and my teaching salary at Johns Hopkins I would be able to get by without giving up my weekend evenings. After all, if one were willing to work for the low wages that college teaching offered, what was the point of relinquishing the leisure time for reading, writing, and thinking that went along with them? If I were ever going back to my original goal of being a newspaperman—and I had not permanently ruled that out— then a copy desk was not the way to do it. So I gave the *Sun* notice. No tears were shed on either side, so far as I know. In the next several years I occasionally wrote articles for the *Sunday Sun Magazine,* and for some years I reviewed books fairly regularly for the editorial page of the *Evening Sun,* but with the enterprises under the managing editorship of Buck Dorsey I had no further traffic.

I thought that my six months or so on the *Sun* would constitute an end to my adventures as a copy editor. As it worked out, however, this was not quite what happened. Two summers later, in 1952, we found ourselves in a financial bind. I had expected to teach a course in summer school for which I would receive an extra stipend, but that depended upon enough students enrolling in freshman English to justify the class. Not enough did. My teaching salary as an instructor remained very low, and my wife, who had been earning a small stipend for teaching a class in political science while working toward her doctorate, would be drawing no pay over the summer.

Washington, D.C., was only forty-five minutes away by train, so I wrote letters to the newspapers there, asking whether they might have need of part-time help to fill in for persons on vacation. In response I received a letter from the managing editor of the *Washington Evening Star* saying that there was a place open on the copy desk for the Sunday edition, and asking me to come over that Saturday evening to try

out. In those days the *Evening Star* was the leading
newspaper in the national capital, publishing six
evenings a week and Sunday morning. The pay would
be $35 a night—which would help mightily in getting
us through the summer, until my wife began being
paid for teaching in the fall.

So I rode over to Washington on the train, showed
up at the office of the *Evening Star,* and was assigned a
place on the rim. There I found myself among as di-
lapidated an aggregation of aging journalists as ever I
had encountered in a newsroom. There were a half-
dozen persons in position around the desk. Except for
the slot man, who looked to be in his forties, not one
could have been less than sixty years old, and most appeared older than that. I am reminded of Nathaniel
Hawthorne's description, in "The Custom House," of
the old-timers he discovered gathered about the wood
stove when he arrived to assume his post as surveyor
of the Port of Salem:

> They were ancient sea-captains, for the most
> part, who, after being tost on every sea, and
> standing up sturdily against life's tempestuous
> blast, had finally drifted into this quiet nook;
> where, with little to disturb them, except the
> periodical terrors of a presidential election, they
> one and all acquired a new lease of existence.
> Though by no means less liable than their fellow-

men to age and infirmity, they had some talis-
man or other that kept death at bay.

The slot man showed me the various headline
sizes, then placed a story in the wire basket for my editing. I read through it, marked it up as needed, put a
headline on it, and handed it back, whereupon I was
given another, which I also edited and headlined.
Then came another, and another, and so on through
the evening.

I worked away on story after story, lengthy or brief,
editing the copy, writing the headlines. I was somewhat surprised to find myself handling several of the
longer and more prominently featured local stories;
usually a new man on a copy desk was given only
lesser stories. When finally all the pages were closed
and I was free to depart, it was well after 1 A.M.

I took a taxicab over to the Union Station, bought
a copy of the Sunday edition of the paper, and
boarded the next train for Baltimore. On the ride
back I looked through the pages of the edition. It had
occurred to me that I was being asked to handle a
large number of stories. What I now saw was that,
with the exception of the sports section and other
sections which had been prepared previously, approximately one of every four news headlines, large or
small, in that edition of the *Sunday Star* had been written by me. I felt a degree of satisfaction in having re-

tained my professional competence after my several years' absence from newsrooms.

A week went by without my hearing further from the *Star*. At length I wrote to ask, and I got back a letter in which the managing editor informed me that he had assumed that when I had not received word I would understand that the job was not mine.

As it turned out, the failure to get the Saturday night job on the *Star*'s copy desk did not produce a financial crisis at home, because unexpectedly a summer-school class opened up for me to teach after all. Still, I wondered what had happened in Washington. I believed that I knew enough about what was involved in copy-editing work to feel reasonably certain that there could have been no complaints about my trial performance on the rim. Neither could my failure to be offered the job have been due to anything that I might have said or done, for other than a query or two as to style I had been kept too busy all evening long to say anything to anybody.

There was always the chance, of course, that someone else had tried out for the position and done better at it than I had. But another possibility occurred to me. To judge from what I had seen that evening, it seemed probable that for the most part the copy editors at work on Saturday night were not those who manned the rim during the week. Except for the Sunday edition, the *Star* was an afternoon paper, and the regulars on the copy desk worked daytime hours. A collection of elderly part-timers may have been employed to work on Saturday nights and thereby pick up a little extra income.

By objective standards my performance had been nothing remarkable; any reasonably efficient newspaper deskman could have matched it. But as it was, I may well have caused some perturbation among those who worked there on Saturday nights. If ever brought to the attention of persons in the business office entrusted with editorial cost-effectiveness, the example I had unwittingly given might suggest that instead of a half-dozen and more graying veterans picking up a little extra money, a couple of somewhat younger, more efficient men from the weekday desk, if made to take turns working on Saturday nights, could handle all the copy editing and headline writing needed, at a considerable saving in salary. Newspaper business managers were renowned for habitually thinking in just such terms.

The managing editor, no spring chicken himself, had doubtless worked alongside and then over most or all of those men when they had been younger. Told by the slot man what had happened, it was conceivable that he had placed friendship before financial calculation, of which there was already far too much in the newspaper profession.

If that was so, then what I should have done was to

have dawdled over each story, nursing it along, handling the writing of the headline as if it were a conundrum to be solved only by painstaking cogitation, and taking care not to hand it back inside of a half hour. Instead, in my innocence I had gone charging in, edited and written headlines to one story after another, paying no attention to what others on the rim were doing.

I do not know for certain that this was what happened. But some years later I learned something that may have borne out my surmise. I was writing book reviews for the *Sunday Star* during the mid- and late 1960s, and one weekend the book editor, Edwin Tribble, came down to Hollins College, Virginia, where I was professor of English, to ask me to consider moving to Washington and becoming the newspaper's book columnist. The editor, Newbold Noyes, he said, thought highly of my work. By that time I was quite certain that I did not want to depart the grooves of academe, not even for a well-paying job in Washington writing three book review columns a week. (Which as it turned out was just as well, because not too many years later the *Star* went out of business. Like almost every other afternoon paper in the country, large and small, it had been done in by television.)

In any event, when the book editor visited me at Hollins, I told him the story about my abortive tryout on the copy desk, and my theory as to why it might have worked out as it did. He smiled. The managing editor in question, he intimated, had been noted for being a very loyal man.

For whatever reason, that single night's work in Washington was the end of my career as a copy editor. I was to have one more whirl at daily journalism before settling permanently into the academy, but it would not involve writing or editing news.

In retrospect it seemed clear that I should never have gone to work on a copy desk in the first place. I may have possessed the requisite technical skills, but not the appropriate temperament for the job. I lacked patience. If being entrusted with putting together the entire edition of a small daily newspaper by myself, headlines, copy editing, layout, news selection, and all, as I had done in Staunton, had proved to be boring after a time, what could I have expected of a job that entailed editing news stories, writing headlines, and nothing else? But at the time I had needed the money, and copy editing was a decent-paying trade.

The copy desk as I knew it back when news was written on typewriters and set into slugs of hot metal letters by linotype operators exists as such no more. Computerized phototypesetting has changed everything. No cluster of elderly copy editors gather around

the rim of a U-shaped desk. Instead there are rows of
men and women—and the latter are now fully as
much a part of the news operations as the men—who
function in small groups as teams together with reporters and designers. They can be found peering into
computer screens, editing and running spelling checks
on stories, then passing them along to designers who
fit them into place on computerized page layouts and
write headlines. Back and forth along the electronic
circuits the stories move, inspected en route by various editors.

No longer is a story's headlining and progression
into print entrusted principally to the graying, the
balding, the soon-to-be-retired, the kicked-upstairs.
Younger people who have been specifically trained to
edit news and to design pages are now very much involved. The swiftness of computerized technology is
combined with the painstaking word-by-word analysis
of individual editing to produce a daily newspaper
that, although at first it may resemble those of a half
century ago, gets into its finished form by a process
that is far more complex, and more efficient, than
anything attempted in my time in the newsroom.

Is the finished product better? Better written, better edited, better designed, more newsworthy than the
newspapers I once worked for? Of course it is. Not
only that, but it had damn well better be. The commu-

nications medium against which newspapers are now in daily combat can, in swiftness and graphic vividness, outperform them with ease. To hold their own and to flourish, the daily newspapers of our own time must bring to the presentation of news those qualities of thoroughness, authenticity, and intelligence that the hasty improvisation and the built-in need to simplify everything of even the best television news coverage cannot offer.

So there is little place for smugness on newspapers anymore, and no place for the institutionalized toleration of stodginess—not when the microfilm rooms of research libraries are stacked with the now-forgotten files of daily papers that once seemed to enjoy a permanent status in every local household.

Still, what was very good then can stand up as very good in comparison with anything today, because human beings wrote and continue to write news stories and compose headlines, and unlike technology, the human capabilities—the excellences that make first-rate journalists what they are—have not changed, but only been adjusted to a different circumstance.

In any event, from all that I have seen, daily newspaper work remains a highly useful profession. The changes it has undergone have been largely for the better. As for the old-fashioned copy desk that flourished in the days of my youth, from what I remember of its operations, and to the extent that my experience was representative, I cannot say that its decline and fall are greatly to be lamented.

\#   \#   \#

7

Almost up to the last minute the evidence was available. The trouble was that I did not want to listen. In particular a telephone conversation sticks in my mind.

In September of 1955 I had agreed to go down to Richmond and be associate editor of the afternoon newspaper, the *News-Leader,* beginning in January, and meanwhile I was writing three editorials a week from Philadelphia. Sometime in November I wrote a piece about the fall season, on how the leaves were turning sallow and the chill was spreading and there was death in the air.

When several days later I received in the mail the issue of the *News-Leader* in which it appeared, I found that the editor, Jack Kilpatrick, had rewritten it to emphasize the crispness and the fall colors and the pumpkins and cider and so on, and eliminated the death-in-the-air motif. "That's not the way I feel about the fall," Kilpo had said when we talked on the telephone, as we did several times a week.

Which should have told me that it would never work. But I did not wish to hear. I was looking forward to a triumphal—as far as I was concerned—return to what had been my lifelong career ambition, and to the South where I had grown up and wished to live and work. In Philadelphia, at the University of Pennsylvania, I had felt like a wanderer in a strange land; or, less elegantly, a tropical southern catfish swimming around in a cold-water pond.

To explain what was involved, it is necessary to recapitulate. A year at the Johns Hopkins Writing Seminars had stretched out into six, during which I taught full-time, edited a critical review, and in my final year and almost as an afterthought, picked up a doctorate. I had also become thoroughly involved in the literature of the then-contemporary South, which at that time was not considered a fully reputable subject for capital-S Scholarship. I had made friends with some of the poets and critics who had developed the Southern Agrarian movement of the late 1920s and early 1930s—Allen Tate, John Crowe Ransom, Donald

Davidson, Robert Penn Warren, Cleanth Brooks—and who, unlike most of the Ph.D.-accredited scholars who taught southern literature, were thoroughly interested in what contemporary southern poets, novelists, and critics were writing. In so doing I had also picked up a supply of conservative social and political theory which comported awkwardly with my New Deal/Fair Deal views. (As indeed was true for Robert Penn Warren as well.)

In July of 1954 I became executive secretary of the American Studies Association, a learned society which had received a three-year Carnegie developmental grant and whose headquarters were at the University of Pennsylvania. It carried with it an assistant professorship of American civilization, without teaching duties. Essentially what I did was to work with scholars in various parts of the country in setting up regional American Studies groups. A great deal of travel was necessary, which enabled me as a card-carrying railroad buff to make trips on trains from coast to coast. What I was in effect was a Visiting Academic Rotarian.

The American literature scholar under whose auspices I had been brought to Pennsylvania, Robert E. Spiller, was a heartening contrast to the pedantry and academic snobbishness I had encountered in the Johns Hopkins English Department, but as chairman of the American Civilization program at Penn he had made a crucial error in arranging for my appointment. The program itself was interdisciplinary, with the faculty drawn from a number of university departments. Before hiring me, Spiller had failed to ask the approval of the chairman of the English Department, and since that gentleman conducted his department along the same lines as Captain William Bligh did HMS *Bounty,* there would be no chance of my being allowed to teach any literature courses. Inasmuch as it was literature, American and otherwise, that I was most interested in, that constituted a severe limitation to any future prospects for me at Penn.

I was tired of temporary situations and year-to-year appointments. I had held three newspaper jobs in two years, then at Johns Hopkins a series of one-year instructorships, without any prospect for promotion and tenure. Now I was in a position funded by a foundation grant that would run out in three years. I had not yet begun looking for another position when Jack Kilpatrick had approached me about coming back to Richmond as associate editor—i.e., as editorial writer No. 2.

I had known Kilpo for several years, had written a weekly book column for his page for a time, and I enjoyed his company. He had a splendid sense of humor, and I admired his writing skills. My wife and I also liked Jack's wife, Marie, a talented artist. Although I did not share his ultraconservative political views, these were not allowed to intrude upon his personal relationships.

During my vacation in the summer of 1955 I went down for a week's tryout. I enjoyed being back on a newspaper, and in Richmond, where I had friends on the staff and family in the city. I liked going down into a composing room again and working with printers, and writing editorials in which I could say what I thought about various matters (not politics, however, for that was Kilpo's bailiwick). In general it felt good to be part once again of an ongoing daily newspaper operation. It what I had always intended to do with my life, or so I thought. As for Kilpo, he was interesting to work with—as indeed he remained during all the time that I worked with him. I had a fine time. I was interviewed by the Fourth Floor—the term covered the Richmond Newspapers' publisher, general manager, director of research, and whoever was engaged in overseeing the general operations—and was offered the associate editor's job, at a salary of $7,000, or $1,500 more than I was earning in Philadelphia. After only brief deliberation I accepted the offer, to become effective January 1, 1956. Until then, I would write several editorials a week from Philadelphia.

Not long after I agreed to go to Richmond, the

Carnegie Corporation awarded the American Studies Association a second three-year grant, and Robert Spiller asked me to reconsider my decision. I would be assured of at least four more years on the job, be given a course to teach, and thereafter involved more in the American Civilization program as each year went by. And if, as Spiller pointed out, by the time the second grant expired I did not wish to stay on at Penn, I would surely be in an excellent position to move into an appointment teaching literature at another university.

It was good advice, but I would have none of it. I did not care for the University of Pennsylvania and living in suburban Philadelphia. Other than Spiller, who was more than twice my age, I had found no congenial colleagues on the faculty. Nobody there was interested in southern literature and history.

The truth was that in the seven years since I had left Richmond and the Associated Press to live in the North—and Baltimore and Philadelphia were both northern as far as I was concerned—I had built up in my mind an idyllic Never-Never-Land of romance and glamour, compounded out of the Confederate tradition, the polemical writings of the Southern Agrarians, memories of childhood, and recollections of the less frantic, less impersonal ways of small-city southern life of an earlier time. The whole was steeped in nostalgia for a Land of Lost Content, and I had called this imagined place the South.

I had even rationalized myself into believing—more accurately, into thinking I believed—that southern racial arrangements were something other than the flagrant injustice they were to black southerners. I don't think I was really a segregationist, but such was my sense of alienation from the urban metropolitan milieu which I now found myself inhabiting that I had managed to persuade myself that the recent *Brown v. Board of Education* decision of the Supreme Court was—well, not so much wrong as premature, too far ahead of its time. Such was the power of nostalgia and the wish to Go Home Again.

Meanwhile the *Richmond News-Leader,* with the enthusiastic encouragement of its management, was mounting an all-out campaign advocating Massive Resistance to racial integration. Jack Kilpatrick was writing what can only be characterized as a brilliantly wrongheaded series of editorials in advocacy of something known as Interposition, whereby in accordance with the resolutions of the Virginia and Kentucky legislatures of the 1790s in opposition to the Alien and Sedition Acts, Virginia and the other southern states were to "interpose" their sovereignty between the federal government and laws they considered unconstitutional. Theoretically it wasn't outright Nullification,

such as John C. Calhoun and the South Carolina legislature had proclaimed in 1832 until Andrew Jackson
had called their bluff. Then what was it? Nobody was
quite clear.

That fall I had gone down to Richmond for a
week to get out the editorial page while the Kil-
patricks took a much-deserved vacation. At that time
the Byrd Organization, the state political machine
controlled by U.S. Senator Harry F. Byrd, was engaged
in promoting a plan that would supposedly thwart the
mandatory integration of public schools by permitting
localities to assign pupils to schools individually on a
basis that would be "nonracial," and by offering tuition
grants for the families of students not wanting to attend integrated schools. Kilpo had written a series of
editorials in advocacy, which were used each day while
I was filling in for him.

By the time we moved down to Richmond in January, however, Interposition had taken over and the
earlier plan was being junked, despite a statewide ref-
erendum that approved it. It was to be Massive Resistance all the way, with Harry Byrd calling the tune and
the *News-Leader* blowing the charge six afternoons
each week.

So, after seven years of academia, I was returning to
the vocation I had coveted when young—and what is

more, working at it alongside one of the most remarkable and capable newspaper editors of that or any
time. Having succeeded Douglas Southall Freeman as
editor of a thriving afternoon newspaper with a circulation in six figures, James Jackson Kilpatrick had
quickly made his impact on the Virginia scene. In
years to come, as the author of a syndicated column
and as a television personality, he would become a nationally known commentator. In the Richmond area
almost nobody was neutral about Kilpo, as I soon discovered.

In my office at the University of Pennsylvania I
had kept on display a pair of portraits of Robert E.
Lee and Stonewall Jackson in elaborate gold-paint-
gilded frames, and upon arriving in Richmond I
brought them down to the *News-Leader* editorial offices. Kilpo was delighted; up they went on the wall of
the front office for all to see.

Within a day or two after I began work as associate
editor I wrote an editorial which began, "The people
of Virginia have spoken," or something to that effect,
and proceeded to endorse the continued segregation
of schools. Jack Kilpatrick did not use it—for which
decision I soon had reason to be profoundly grateful.
For it took me only a couple of days of observing the
state legislature in session to begin to realize that what
I had been trying to do was to rationalize myself into

a defense of the indefensible. In the editorial that I wrote, and all during the preceding fall and now winter, I had in effect been arguing with myself, trying to convince myself that I believed what I did not believe and advocated what I did not advocate. Fortunately for me, none of it got into print, so that afterward I could feel that at least I had not actively contributed to the destructive work, however discreditable my intentions may have been.

On one occasion, several months earlier when I had been out traveling in Louisiana and western Tennessee on American Studies Association business, there had been a lynching in Mississippi, and I had fired off an editorial condemning it. Kilpo had not published it; he would not, he said, add to the burden of the people of Mississippi in their time of agony. In short, he was not going to let his editorial page be used to censure the South, no matter what. That alone should have made me realize what I was engaged in trying to do: to convince myself that in the idyllic South that I wanted to believe existed, there was no toleration for acts of racial brutality, and if such crass things did take place, all responsible citizens, public and private, would at once arise to denounce the deed and punish the perpetrators. I should have been able to see that what had happened in Mississippi was possible only because one law existed for whites and another for blacks, and that to maintain segregation the Best People could be counted on to look the other way when as a direct result of legally institutionalized racial discrimination the Lower Orders indulged themselves in mayhem.

To repeat, I should have been able to see that, but as long as I had been resident in distant places like Philadelphia, Pa., it had been possible to pretend otherwise. Now I was back in the South, in the Commonwealth of Virginia, where the rhetoric was somewhat more genteel and lynchings were not tolerated, but where at the time of my return the General Assembly of Virginia was engaged in enacting laws that would automatically shut down any public school system to which black children were admitted. Once on the scene, it would not take long for my vision to improve.

Each day after writing an editorial, overseeing the making up of the editorial page and the adjoining op-ed page in the composing room, and performing whatever other chores were mine to do, I walked over to the State Capitol, took a seat in the press gallery, and watched the progress of Interposition. Overlooking the proceedings up in the House of Delegates were a number of black Virginians—professional people, academics, attorneys, whatever—who looked on while assorted white legislators spouted assorted varieties of nonsense about them. In particular I was im-

pressed with the asininity of the biblical arguments
being solemnly advanced by Delegate John B. Boatwright,
whose brother had been president of the University of
Richmond when I had studied there. This man, the
logic of whose argument would have insulted the spiel
of a purveyor of snake oil at a tent show, went on at
length to "prove" the biblical case for racial segregation. Had the year been 1856 instead of 1956 he
would have used the identical evidence to defend
chattel slavery.

There was in the General Assembly a group of legislators, mainly from northern Virginia and Richmond,
who were doing their best to keep the state from carrying out Senator Harry Byrd's orders to get the
statutes on the books for dismantling the public
schools rather than integrating them. Fully aware that
a majority of the voters who elected the Delegates to
the Assembly were opposed to integration, as sensible
politicians they were basing their arguments to their
fellow Delegates not on the injustice of segregation or
the merits of racial integration, but on the vital need
to safeguard public education and to obey the Law of
the Land. We don't want to integrate the schools, either, their argument went, but if doing so is the only
way to preserve our public school system, then we
must be prepared, however reluctantly, to do it, for our
children's right to an education should come before
anything else.

I got an informative lesson in the common-sense practicality of the academic community of which I had so recently been part when a delegation from Charlottesville and the faculty of the University of Virginia arrived to testify at a hearing. One after another they proceeded to instruct the legislature about the damage done to the psyches of black children by racial discrimination, the insidious nature of racism, the virtues of equality of educational opportunity, and so on. All of which was quite true, but to those legislators engaged in battling desperately to block the closing of the public schools, and whose only chance lay in making the cause of preserving public education seem more urgent than that of keeping schools segregated, it was not at all the note they wished to have sounded at that juncture. As one young legislator, Fitzgerald Bemiss, told me out in the hallway, "They're killing us in there."

The fight of Jerry Bemiss and the handful of other state senators and delegates was probably doomed to begin with, but in undercutting what the legislative defenders of the public schools were battling to achieve, the Charlottesville group's testimony played wonderfully into the hands of the advocates of segregation-at-any-price. At least one result of the failure of the moderates to block Harry Byrd's program of Massive Resistance in the General Assembly during those first several weeks after I moved back to Richmond was the shutting down, less than two years later, of the public schools in Prince Edward County, Virginia, and the denial of education to the black children of that county for three full years.

As for my fond pastorale of a southern garden in the desert of urban industrial America, it had received its first serious check at the hands of reality. Several years would go by before I accepted the full implications of what I now began to learn, but the process was under way whereby I came to realize that the South to which I thought I was moving back had in important respects been constructed along the same lines as the place that the Richmond novelist James Branch Cabell described his elders as having created in the latter decades of the nineteenth century: "an Old South which had died proudly at Appomattox without ever having been besmirched by the wear and tear of existence." Whether in Philadelphia, Richmond, Charleston, or Trebizond, there could be no escape from living in the modern world.

Jack Kilpatrick's editorial style in the *News-Leader* was very different from that of his counterpart Virginius Dabney in the morning *Times-Dispatch*—as different, indeed, as the two editors' backgrounds and personalities. Kilpo was young, a westerner by birth and rearing, without inherited social credentials, outspoken and assertive. Dabney was everything that Kilpo wasn't: a member of an illustrious Virginia family of plantation ancestry, in his late fifties in those years, very much a part of the Richmond Establishment socially, and moderate in his conservativism and his manner. In the 1920s he had been a disciple of H. L. Mencken, and in the 1930s a New Dealer. During the war years he had ruffled local feathers by campaigning editorially for an end to the law forcing black people to ride in the rear of city streetcars and buses.

In 1948, when it still seemed barely possible to be both a southern liberal and a segregationist, he had won a Pulitzer Prize for his editorial writing. But as the battle lines over civil rights took shape in the years after World War II, his political views, like those of the Richmond Establishment in general, became more conservative. Even so, they were not sufficiently conservative to suit the general manager of Richmond Newspapers, Inc., John Dana Wise, with whom Dabney clashed repeatedly. With the publisher, Tennant Bryan, he got along much better, despite Bryan's equally fierce conservatism, but Massive Resistance was not for him, so that while he remained editor, the *Times-Dispatch*'s editorials supporting all-out defiance of the Supreme Court's rulings outlawing racial segregation were written by K. V. Hoffman, a columnist and associate editor who held ultraconservative views

similar to Bryan's. While Hoffman could match Kilpo's
political attitudes, he lacked Kilpo's vivacity and in-
ventiveness, and it was the *News-Leader*'s editorial page
that kept the animals stirred up.

As an editorial writer I was not permitted to write
anything having to do with politics, whether national,
state, or local. That was Kilpo's territory—which was
agreeable to me, for my politics and his were different
up and down the line. What I could and did write
about was foreign affairs, about any aspects of government that were without political ramifications, about
history, about literature, about higher education, about
the behavior of cats, about the traffic in downtown
Richmond, about sports, about television, about the
weather, about music, and so on—anything, in other
words, that was not of major importance. Before I arrived there had been a local woman employed to
write about foreign policy, but that subject was now
assigned to me. The only explanation that I can think
of for the readiness to allow me to call the shots in that
realm is that both Kilpo and the publisher were so absorbed in domestic politics that what went on beyond
the national borders was of secondary interest to them.

I tended to be an internationalist in such matters.
In those days foreign policy was still largely bipartisan.
Both Richmond newspapers were anti-Communist, of

course, but McCarthyism and domestic witch-hunting were politically dead by then, with General Eisenhower now President Eisenhower and very much in charge in Washington—much more so, indeed, than most people realized at the time. When in 1956 Great Britain, France, and Israel collaborated in an attack on Egypt, which under Gamal Nasser had nationalized the Suez Canal and assumed the lead in Arab militancy, the Eisenhower administration condemned their action, and I joined in with an editorial entitled "Britannia Waives the Rules." In Europe, in Latin America, in the Far East I had the United States actively supporting the United Nations, NATO, Pan-Americanism, and the like. As it worked out, for several years after my tenure in Richmond the *News-Leader* could be seen crawling back off the limbs on which I had placed it.

As editor, Kilpo had certain pet projects which he asked me to take over—always, I hasten to add, provided that I could do so in good conscience, for at no time was I ever instructed in what to say about any issue or asked to write anything that I did not myself believe. One project had to do with the State Milk Commission. Although the day had passed when the economy of the Commonwealth of Virginia was primarily agricultural in nature, it was nonetheless governed by an Organization that relied heavily upon the votes of a rural and small-town constituency to keep it in power. (This was before the U.S. Supreme Court had issued its one-person, one-vote ruling that ended the domination of southern state legislatures by the rural counties through markedly disproportionate representation.) To ensure that the price of milk would be placed at a level profitable to dairy farmers, the Milk Commission was empowered to set retail prices throughout the state.

A retail chain in the northern Virginia area had challenged the commission's powers by selling milk in large containers at considerably reduced prices, which delighted consumers having young children to feed, but the Milk Commission had prevailed. When Kilpo first became editor of the *News-Leader* the artificially pegged prices had annoyed him considerably, so he began tearing into the Milk Commission's operations editorially, to the satisfaction of urban housewives and the retail chain which had sought to sell milk in bulk at lower prices. The latter took to reprinting Kilpo's anti–Milk Commission editorials as display advertisements in other state newspapers.

Kilpo's objection to the artificial pegging of milk prices seemed reasonable to me, so when he suggested that I take up the cause, I was willing. I examined what had been written on the subject, and wrote an editorial beginning with a statement that I hoped would be read as comic hyperbole: "If this were a free country, there would be no Milk Commission."

The next day the editorial was used to lead off the page. After I had gone to the composing room and overseen the makeup, I walked on down to the State Capitol to see what was going on that day. There I ran into the star political reporter for the *News-Leader* and the best newspaper reporter I have ever known, my close friend Guy Friddell.

Guy and I had finished up together at the University of Richmond after the war and had kept very much in touch thereafter. He had put in a spell as Kilpo's associate editor not long before I had, but editorial writing had not proved to be to his taste—not on the *News-Leader,* at any rate, for not only were his political and social views directly contrary to Kilpo's and the management's, but what went on politically in the Commonwealth of Virginia meant a great deal more to him than it did to me. So he had returned to the news side, which welcomed him back.

Guy had the ability to get along with politicos of all persuasions, and to earn their friendship and trust for his absolute nonpartisanship as a reporter of news. On one occasion a few years later, after I had left Richmond and newspapering, I happened to be in town during the midst of a furious gubernatorial campaign and dropped by his house about 8 P.M. to find Ted Dalton, the Republican candidate for governor who was bitterly opposed editorially by the *News-Leader,* eating a late dinner with him. Senator Harry

Byrd, whose views on racial matters were anathema to Guy, once singled him out among a gathering of reporters, saying: "This is the best one of all of you." (A few years later, upon becoming editor of the editorial page of the *Norfolk Virginian-Pilot,* Guy tore into Massive Resistance, racial discrimination, and the Byrd Organization with everything he had. Shortly before he took over in Norfolk, Senator Byrd called him aside at a reception in Washington. Since Guy would now be writing editorials for an anti-Organization paper, he would necessarily have to oppose what Byrd stood for, the senator said, and he was not ever to let their personal friendship inhibit him from writing what he thought.)

To return to the Milk Commission, on the day in question, after I had encountered Guy at the Capitol, he proposed that we have lunch at Grunewald's Restaurant two blocks away. Numerous people who had business at the Capitol and various nearby office buildings dined at Grunewald's, and when we entered a group of men already seated at a table hailed Guy. There were introductions all around, and it was proposed that we join them. As we did, it dawned upon me who it was that we were about to have lunch with—the members of the Virginia Milk Commission. Guy had introduced me only as associate editor, not as Kilpo's co-worker.

I looked at my watch. The first edition of the *News-Leader* would begin rolling off the presses in approximately twenty-five minutes. Copies would be delivered to newsboys in and about the downtown area not long afterward, but with luck I should be able to finish lunch before any of the commission members got hold of one and read my editorial—which, to repeat, began with the ringing assertion, "If this were a free country, there would be no Milk Commission."

We ordered lunch, it was duly delivered, and I began eating mine while listening to Guy and the various members of the commission as they conversed about various things, none of them having to do with the price of milk. All was going well until out of the corner of my eye I noticed a newspaper vendor come through the front door with a bundle of copies of the *News-Leader* under his arm. "Well, I've got to be going," I announced.

"Don't run off," Guy told me. "What did you write about today?" (Like the members of the Milk Commission, he had not yet seen the first edition.)

"Oh, nothing much," I said. "Foreign policy." Which was true, for the editorial about the Milk Commission had been composed the previous afternoon. All the while I kept my eye on the vendor, who was moving from table to table.

No more than a couple of minutes went by before the newsboy neared us, and one of the members of the commission beckoned to him. The newsboy came over and several of our luncheon companions purchased copies and began opening them.

I leaped to my feet. "I'm sorry, but I've got to run. I'm late for an appointment! I enjoyed meeting you gentlemen." I handed Guy a couple of dollars. "You get the check," I told him. "I'll see you later." And I hurried out of the restaurant and onto Broad Street.

Later that afternoon, back at the office, I asked Guy what had happened when they saw the editorial. "All they said was 'I see Kilpatrick's after us again,'" he reported.

There was a sequel. Several years after I had left the *News-Leader,* either Kilpo or his associate editor at the time underwent a change of heart about the Milk Commission and decided that it wasn't such a bad idea after all, since it prevented the smaller dairies and individual dairy farmers from being driven to the wall by large out-of-state operations. So an editorial was published supporting the commission and its activities. Whereupon the chain that had been battling for the right to sell milk in larger containers at low prices took out a sizable advertisement featuring my editorial and the more recent one side by side, under a headline reading, "YOU WERE RIGHT THE FIRST TIME, RICHMOND NEWS-LEADER!"

Working with Jack Kilpatrick was an education. An

Oklahoman, he had come to the news staff fresh out
of the University of Missouri School of Journalism
during the war years and swiftly shown his mettle as a
police reporter. At that time the editor of the *News-
Leader* was Douglas Southall Freeman, the distinguished Civil War historian and a man of much *gravi-
tas*. Dr. Freeman—he was always referred to as
such—had invited Kilpo to contribute editorials. Six
months later, in 1949, Dr. Freeman retired, and Kilpo,
aetat twenty-eight, was made editor. The approach of
the editorial columns underwent a metamorphosis.
The stately sobriety with which Dr. Freeman had issued his pronouncements upon the state of the uni-
verse and the doings of the Commonwealth gave way
to a cutting and slashing, acerbic, highly readable performance, laced with wit and composed with an ear
for the acuity of the English language that delighted
many and infuriated not a few. There was no doubt as
to where the *Richmond News-Leader* stood editorially
on the issues of the day, or on anything else.

Conservativism for Kilpo was a doctrine, not an attitude, and he professed it with all the diffidence of a
steam locomotive. His prose style was modeled upon
H. L. Mencken's, and when he was at his best, which
was much of the time, he wrote with the roguishness
and exuberance that the Sage of Baltimore had done
in the 1920s. With, however, this difference: the

Mencken of that day could look about him and wreak execution on fools and folly of any sort whatever. Kilpo, by contrast, was committed to one side, and therefore unable to operate with a similar omnipotence. One result was that by no means all of what, under other circumstances, would have been his natural clientele—persons of more than ordinary education capable of recognizing wit, irony, satire, drollery, inspired invective, and farce when they saw it—could properly enjoy his prose.

His chosen clientele in those years, or the portion of it that mattered most, was the Richmond Establishment, as personified in the publisher of the two Richmond newspapers, David Tennant Bryan. A man of learning, a skillful writer himself, with polished manners, very much a Virginia aristocrat as such things go (and they could sometimes go pretty far), Bryan was a businessman, of very conservative views, and he desired his newspapers to echo those views editorially. Let it also be noted, however, that he demanded that a strict division be maintained at all times between editorial opinion and the objective presentation of news. Reporters and news editors in Tennant Bryan's employment had no complaints to make about interference from the Fourth Floor.

From well before the Civil War onward, Richmond had been a financial and industrial center, with the wealth of its First Families based not upon the ownership and cultivation of land but on railroads, banking, manufacturing, medicine, the law, and retail and wholesale commerce. This was the constituency for which the two Richmond newspapers spoke. It was an oligarchy, and bent upon retaining its prerogatives. The children of the Establishment mostly went to private schools; indeed, the willingness of the Virginia leadership to allow the schools to close rather than integrate had its counterpart in the violent post-Reconstruction-era political upheavals of seventy-five years earlier. Richmond had been the citadel of the Funders who, rather than forcing a readjustment of the state's prewar debt in order to keep the schools open, strove to safeguard the financial Honor of Old Virginia at the cost of having no public schools at all.

There was (and still is) a powerful awareness of class and caste; who Belonged and Didn't Belong was important. Certain social institutions existed in which membership was symbolically significant. The male business and social elite of the city lunched at the Commonwealth Club, and the women at the Richmond Woman's Club. Not to belong to these signified that one was not socially Accepted.

Jack Kilpatrick was not invited to join the Commonwealth Club. It was one thing to lead the charge on behalf of what the Richmond Establishment advo-

cated, and another to do so inordinately and to be
from Oklahoma. Neither was Marie Kilpatrick, a
gifted artist and sculptor of Italian descent, asked to
join the Woman's Club. It was important to them, and
it rankled. Decades after he left Richmond, Kilpo told
Earle Dunford, who was writing a history of the
Richmond Newspapers, "The editor of the paper
ought to be a member of the club in Richmond. And
not being admitted to that was a little sting. There was
a little hurt there. And by the same token, Marie
should have been invited to become a member of the
Woman's Club, and she wasn't. Marie was getting pro-
gressively unhappy. She thought she was getting
snubbed." *

At the time when I was working for and with
Kilpo, it would have seemed inconceivable to me that
anyone of his journalistic achievements would care
about whether or not he was asked to join a Richmond social club. But apparently it did. "Richmond
had been very good to me on the whole," he told
Earle Dunford, "but socially I was never there. I was
still the Oklahoma boy." The episode does no credit
to the city of Richmond, Virginia, because whatever
Kilpo's shortcomings, and however one might disagree

* Earle Dunford, *Richmond Times-Dispatch: The Story of a
Newspaper* (Richmond, Va.: Cadmus, 1995).

with his political views, goodness knows that Jack and
Marie Kilpatrick were worth any number of smug,
self-satisfied local citizens of Good Family who may
have considered them mere *arrivistes.*

Kilpo and I got along fine personally. We ate lunch together several times a week, we saw each other in the
evenings from time to time, and during baseball season we spent time together on the third-base line
watching the Richmond Virginians playing in the International League. As an editorial writer I benefitted
considerably from his editing. He could spot an awkward expression or a piece of loose construction, and
with a deft change or two strengthen it.

We also collaborated on projects, sometimes with
unexpected results. There was a move afoot in local
civic circles to open up a large area southeast of the
city along the James River Road for industrial use.
The various local magnates all climbed aboard the
bandwagon. We were talking about it, and it was
agreed that I would write an editorial questioning
why the city needed an industrial park along the
winding, rural James River Road. Didn't we have
plenty of industry as it was? Would the quality of life
of the community benefit or suffer therefrom? So I
wrote the editorial, and Kilpo worked it over a little,
and we published it. Whereupon Kilpo and Tennant

Bryan were deluged with horrified protests, as if we had laid sooty paws upon the Lares and Penates. To question Progress merely for the sake of Progress may have been good conservative doctrine, but not according to the Richmond business community. What it wanted was more and larger payrolls.

On another occasion the Atlantic Coast Line Railroad had decided to move its general offices away from Wilmington, N.C., and Richmond was one of several cities along the route being considered for the relocation. Considerable notice was being taken in the news columns over the visit of a team representing the railroad's management to inspect the city and what it had to offer. We decided to write an ironic piece, tongue in cheek all the way, citing such civic advantages as the going-home automobile traffic along Monument Avenue each evening, the perceptible rise in the air temperature downtown when the General Assembly was in session, the unique aroma of tobacco from the cigarette factories that permeated the atmosphere of the lower city, the domestic advantages of the Virginia Milk Commission, the difficulties of finding a parking place near the Public Library, and other benefits that would accrue to the railroad if it located its offices with us. Our hunch was that the railroad authorities would long since have found out all these things for themselves, that conditions were no worse in Rich-

mond than in any other large city, and that if anything
the humor would be a welcome contrast to the pro-
motional pablum that was otherwise being dished out
to them everywhere they visited. So I wrote a draft,
and Kilpo pointed it up to excellent effect, and the editorial was run while the visiting railroad executives
were in town.

The Chamber of Commerce and the assorted real-
tors of the city were appalled. They didn't consider it
at all amusing. What madness, they asked, could have
overtaken the *News-Leader*? The railroad later decided
not to place its offices in Richmond, but in Jacksonville, Florida. That anything the *News-Leader* had to
say could have had much to do with the decision one
way or the other is improbable; in such matters property tax deferments and real estate easements, not
newspaper editorials, were what counted.

Then there was the Christmas carol opus. Just for
fun, and with Kilpo's abetting, at some point in mid-
December I began to compose an editorial on the
"true" origins of certain well-known holiday carols. It
consisted of a sequence of trumped-up anecdotes. As
for example, a man who commuted from and back to
Ashland, Va., twenty-five miles from town, each
evening, and who on Christmas Eve, instead of catch-
ing his train at the Broad Street Station as usual, lin-
gered for a beer or two or three or four with compan-

ions at a tavern. By the time he arrived home it was very, very late, and his wife Clare, armed with a rolling pin, was awaiting him at the front door. Where have you been? she demanded. The train, he told her, was running far behind its customary schedule: "It came upon the midnight, Clare."

I wrote drafts of five or six such, all with equally bad puns, such as the inattentive little boy who just wouldn't sing out in the youth choir, until at length the choir director became enraged and shouted at him, "Hark thee, Harold Engels! Sing!" Or the couple who were dog fanciers and who entertained their neighbors the Halls, and everyone was very merry until at length a dispute developed into a brawl, and the two couples went at it with all they had. The host ripped a Christmas wreath off the doghouse and commenced to use it as a flail, while his wife shouted, "Deck the Halls with Bowser's holly!"

I turned over my draft to Kilpo to work on, knowing a touch was lacking in the details and that the particular brand of humor that was required was made to order for him. He did not disappoint me. Before he got done with it, my clumsy burlesque had been crafted into a small comic jewel.

It was our thought to use the piece on Christmas Eve, but when Kilpo took the editorial page up to the Fourth Floor for the mandatory review, he returned with word that the burlesque was not to run. There was concern that the piece might be offensive to some readers, and Tennant Bryan wanted it held over for consideration later.

By the time it did appear, during the Christmas season of the year following, I was no longer associate editor of the *News-Leader* but teaching at Hollins College. Kilpo sent me a tearsheet, along with word that there had been a few letters of protest, but that for the most part the piece had caused much merriment and drawn compliments from, among others, several ministerial acquaintances. A decade or so later he revived it in the syndicated column he was by then writing, with due and comic credit to my scholarly researches.

It was not with the occasional collaborative projects that I had difficulty in working with Jack Kilpatrick, but with certain others that I wrote entirely by myself. Like some other editors who as writers have distinctive styles of their own, Kilpo was characteristically unable to acknowledge the distinction between editing something in order to make it more effective on its own terms, which was a useful and necessary editorial function, and reworking it so that it said things the way he would have done had he written it. While this might do when working with the copy of an apprentice writer, with someone of more experience at using the language and a way of saying things on his own it could and did cause trouble. (Characteristically, H. L. Mencken ran into exactly the same difficulties when during the late 1930s he took over temporarily as chief editorial writer for the *Baltimore Evening Sun* and began revising the prose of the other editorial writers.)

What it came down to was that the *Richmond News-Leader's* editorial page was a one-man show, brilliantly done and totally embodying the personality and the prose of its editor. In effect, anyone else writing for it wrote not anonymously but pseudonymously. Kilpo couldn't help it. His makeup was such that anything he did was done virtuoso-style. On one occasion I wrote a piece that centered on a quotation from Shakespeare. I don't recall the subject, but it had nothing to do with politics or any of the other issues on which the *News-Leader* had an established position to maintain. Kilpo proposed to substitute a different Shakespeare quotation for the one I had chosen. This exasperated me. "My God, Kilpo, do we have a policy on Shakespeare?" I asked.

I should have remembered what had happened with the piece I had written about the fall weather, back while I was still in Philadelphia. In truth I had long since asked for it.

Another incident, trivial in itself, irked me. The attorney general of Virginia, J. Lindsay Almond, was a powerful political personality, and at one point he arranged matters so that he was assured of being the Organization candidate for governor, even though Harry Byrd would have preferred someone more docile at the head of the slate. (This would later have important consequences.) Almond's maneuver amused me. At the time there was a Burl Ives song that was much heard on the radio, the chorus of which began "Cindy, oh Cindy, Cindy don't let me down," so just for fun I typed out a parody, with several verses and a chorus that went, "Lindsay, oh Lindsay," etc., and ended "Call me in Washington the next time you're in town." I prefaced it with "*Harry Byrd loquitur*" and entitled it "The Gubernatorial Blues."

Kilpo happened to come into my office shortly afterward, and I showed it to him. "Let's use it!" he proposed at once, much to my surprise, since its implicit meaning was that Virginia's senior U.S. senator, a man he much esteemed, had been outmaneuvered. He made a minor syntactical change or two, which as usual improved it, wrote a decorative head with a couple of musical notes, and it appeared at the bottom of the editorial column the next day.

On Saturdays, when the paper went to press early and there was never much going on, it was our custom to alternate coming in to make up the page, and the following Saturday I happened to be in the office by myself. I was looking for something on the secretary's desk, and I happened to glance down at the carbon copy of a letter and spotted my name. Kilpo must have dictated it to the secretary, who had typed it for his signature but had not yet put the copy in the files. Seeing that my name was being cited, I proceeded to read the letter, which was addressed to Senator Harry Byrd. Attached to it was a letter from the senator saying that he had gotten a chuckle out of "The Gubernatorial Blues," which he thought very cleverly written, and was placing it in his scrapbook to keep as a memento. In reply Kilpo had explained that the parody had been written not by himself but by me, "though I confess," he added, "that I touched it up a bit."

He *had* touched it up, but in his capacity as editor, not author. Nor had he shown me the letter in praise of my parody. If I had not happened to glance down at the secretary's desk and noticed my name on the carbon copy, I should never have known of it.

Still, in justice to Kilpo, there were not one but two egos involved in our working together, for certainly I was not without my own supply of that item. I had come to work with him knowing that what I wrote would by its very nature not ever be bylined. Editorial anonymity was one thing, however, and having everything I wrote made to reflect someone else's personality, no matter how gifted that person was as a journalist, was something else again. I had not bargained for that—and neither, as it turned out, had a sequence of other associate editors who were to follow me in the job, and who came one by one, wrote editorials, mostly enjoyed working with Kilpo on a personal basis, learned from him, but grew impatient with the pseudonymity and departed.

Kilpo took too much pride in his page to be willing to put up with the kind of editorial hack who would write bland pieces about routine matters. On one occasion, back when I was still living in Baltimore and writing a weekly book column for Kilpo, I was in town and went by to have lunch with him. At the time he had someone filling in temporarily as his associate, and as we left the building en route to a restaurant Kilpo was fuming. It seems that the fill-in had turned in an editorial on the subject "Have you checked the electric wiring in your house recently?"

He went looking for associates who had ideas and a flair for writing. The difficulty was that while they may not have been as good at his trade as he was— very few could be that—they were sufficiently talented that they had evolved their own way of saying things. When as head editor he began substituting his style for theirs, they didn't like it. In Earle Dunford's words, "Kilpatrick had a succession of associates on the editorial page who went on to establish names for themselves elsewhere—generally in writing." Guy Friddell was first, followed by myself. After I left there were Jack Hamilton, Richard Whalen, James Lucier, and Garry Wills. Though I say so who shouldn't, that was a pretty impressive crowd. Hamilton was the son of the *News-Leader*'s managing editor, Charles Hamilton, and after his stint with Kilpo went on to the *New York Times* and then to a distinguished career as a journalist and television producer. The last three in that lineup, Whalen, Lucier, and Wills, were conservatives. Kilpo had formed ties with some of the right-of-center groups and publications such as *Current Events,* and these had taken to recommending bright young men to him. All three went on to successful writing careers.

Between the day I joined the *News-Leader* as associate editor and the day that I left to return to teaching, sixteen months went by. For at least the latter half of that span I knew that I was going to leave, and I daresay that Kilpo and Tennant Bryan knew it, too, and were waiting for me to say the word. Although there could be no legitimate complaint about the amount of editorial writing I was doing—Kilpo kept a monthly log of how many column inches of copy each of us contributed, and quantitatively at least I could hold my own—I was certainly not in sympathy with the Richmond Newspapers' political goals, as by rights I should have been. Since Kilpo was writing all the political editorials anyway, my heresy probably did not create any practical difficulties. Still, had my attitude toward politics and racial segregation been other than it was, I might have chipped in with more assistance of an ideological sort from time to time. As it was, on the issues that he and Tennant Bryan cared most about I was of no use whatever.

When I joined the *News-Leader* in 1956 I doubt that either Kilpo or the powers that be believed that they were getting a full-dress conservative, though at the time I was still much taken with some of the views of the Nashville Agrarians. In any event, by the time I had been on the scene for a few months most of the political conservatism that I might have absorbed in reaction to my residence in Pennsylvania had evaporated. During the 1956 presidential campaign the Democratic candidate, Adlai Stevenson, had been photographed with a hole worn in the sole of one of his shoes, and this became a symbol of his campaign. I stopped by Democratic Party headquarters and purchased a silver pin showing the holed shoe. It was the publisher's custom to invite the editorial staffs of the newspapers to lunch on the Fourth Floor every two weeks or so, and the next time I was asked I wore the pin on the lapel of my coat. No comments were forthcoming.

It could only have been annoying to the Fourth Floor to know that the afternoon paper's associate ed-itor, employed in order to voice opinions in print, held views that were directly contradictory to the an-nounced editorial policy. After all, there I was, an avowed Democrat who favored Adlai Stevenson for president, writing for a newspaper which considered the Republican incumbent, Dwight D. Eisenhower, to be too liberal to support, and instead endorsed T. Coleman Andrews, ex–U.S. commissioner of Internal Revenue and now the token presidential candidate of an ultraconservative party of some sort. (Had there been any real danger of Eisenhower's not carrying Vir-ginia, the *News-Leader* would have supported him, as the *Times-Dispatch* was doing.)

No one, not even Tennant Bryan, ever directly re-buked me for my opinions and allegiances. The nearest Bryan came to it was on an occasion when Kilpo was away and I had carried the editorial proof up to him to examine. The next day was St. Patrick's Day, and I had written a humorous piece, or so I thought, in which two Irishmen were talking about how all the important figures in Richmond history had been Irish. The whole thing was patterned on Finley Peter Dunne's "Mr. Dooley" pieces of the 1890s and early

1900s, one of which, centered on the onetime Confederate general Fitzhugh Lee, who had been appointed major general of U.S. volunteers at the time of the war with Spain, opened with the line, "Iv coorse, he's Irish!" The two Irishmen proceeded to run down the local list. In addition to legitimate Irish names such as Dooley, McGuire, McCarthy, and Mayo, they began converting numerous prominent Richmond names into their Irish equivalents. Daniel was made into O'-Daniel, Harrison into Harrigan, Langhorne into Lanahan, Patrick Henry into O'Henry, Morton Thalheimer into Martin Toole Himer, Joseph Bryan into O'Brien, and so on—the last named being Tennant Bryan's grandfather. (Mr. Dooley had regularly referred to William Jennings Bryan—no relation—as William J. O'Brien.)

The piece was devoid of any political significance whatever, and intended as a gentle spoof that nobody could possibly take seriously. Tennant Bryan, however, did not approve. Jokes about people's names, he told me, were not funny. So something else had to be substituted in its place.

As I was leaving his office he handed me a printed flyer. "I'd like for you to read this," he told me. When I got back to my desk I examined it. It was a right-wing attack on state socialism in Sweden, expressed in terms that were simplistic and reductive. Obviously a man of

Tennant Bryan's intellectual sophistication realized that. Giving it to me to read was his way of saying to me, "This is the way you're supposed to be thinking in your position."

As for myself, as the months went by I felt more and more like a kind of hired gun, employed to express opinions on an editorial page that on the key issues of the day was articulating positions with which I was in almost total disagreement. Not only that, but that editorial page was eagerly read and widely admired precisely *for* its political views. The editorials that I wrote were at best marginal to its importance and largely irrelevant to its existence. It upset me, too, when on occasion, in wading in against the proponents of civil rights and school desegregation in the South, Kilpo sometimes attacked friends of mine, including my teacher C. Vann Woodward. Certainly he had the right to criticize those who disagreed with his editorial stance, but it put me in an embarrassing position.

So, the longer I stayed on the job, the less comfortable I felt. I disapproved of what the newspaper of which I was associate editor stood for, I was aware that I wasn't giving Kilpo the kind of help he needed, or enough of it, and I knew that the publisher was not pleased with my performance. For my part I was disenchanted with the whole operation, and with myself most of all.

In returning to Richmond and the newspaper career that I had always intended to follow, I had been determined to maintain my scholarly interest in literature and in particular southern literature. I wanted to continue to write essays and reviews for the literary magazines and quarterly reviews, and to take part in the annual meetings of learned societies. I also hoped to write fiction. During the sixteen months of my tenure in Richmond I wrote several essays, including an overall study, published in the *Journal of Southern History,* of the historical dimensions of southern literature. I also gave scholarly papers at several meetings and at universities. I could see no inherent contradiction in writing newspaper editorials and also doing critical and scholarly writing. After all, both Virginius Dabney and Douglas Southall Freeman had managed both.

As might have been anticipated, however, there were practical problems involved. The responsibility for producing my share of the editorial contents of a daily newspaper meant that as a rule I had to turn out two pieces a day, one of them lengthy, the other brief. After a time I began to realize that I was thinking about everything that happened to me in terms of how it might be written about. If I watched a jet plane arch a contrail high over the western city as I drove home, I wrote about the unexpected sight. If our dog escaped out into the snow at night and wouldn't come in, I wrote about the recalcitrant ways of pupdogs. If we ate a mediocre dinner in an Italian restaurant, I wrote about the scarcity of good Italian cuisine south of Washington and east of New Orleans. If I read a biography of Jelly Roll Morton, I wrote about the origins of New Orleans jazz. And so on. The unrelenting requirements of space to fill on a daily deadline was causing me to experience my life as if it were meant to be converted forthwith into print, which in turn meant that I was seizing upon whatever was immediate and obvious, without giving myself time to let new thoughts and emotions modify and be modified by what had come before.

Related to this was the feeling, on subjects that I cared most about such as literature and history, that I was writing on the surface. The nature of the daily editorial format was inhibiting me from communicating the complexity of a topic. Whatever I wished to say about something, no matter how complicated, had to be expressed in two double-spaced typewritten pages or thereabouts. One must not bore the audience by becoming too technical or pedantic, or confuse it by requiring specialized knowledge about anything. No matter how much time I might spend looking into a topic, the result had to be boiled down to what would fit appropriately into an editorial of six hundred words.

That this was useful training, that it prevented the lazy reliance upon jargon to avoid working out what one really meant to say, was undeniable. Yet there were important matters, aspects of one's experience, that could not be explained in six hundred words.

The essence of writing editorials for newspapers was making what one knew available to a general audience. It was an indispensable function, and to be done effectively required much skill. But what I liked most to do as a writer was not that, but something else. I liked to explore complexity, to search out and develop nuances and gradations. On subjects that were important to me I did not want to stop at a certain point and move on to another topic.

Perhaps if I had been writing on politics and government, and been allowed to develop my thoughts and opinions about that, it would have been different. I might then have gone into the subject on a daily basis, at greater length, and spent much of my time reading about it, finding out more and more about it. Moreover, if the subject was politics I could probably have assumed more detailed knowledge on the part of readers. In that case, when writing editorials I might have set my goal as that of making my readership see and understand how complex were the problems of governing the nation, and the ramifications of the political choices they faced. That was what any responsible newspaper editor did, or tried to do. It was what Kilpo did so well, even if I did not agree with either his premises or conclusions.

Yet supposing I was capable of doing that, how could I possibly do so in my present job? I couldn't even write any of the political editorials, and even if I could have I would have been totally unable to accommodate my opinions to those of the publisher.

So if I intended to continue with the career of newspaper journalist that I had first set out to follow, strayed away from after going off to graduate school, then rejoined via the *Richmond News-Leader,* I had three obvious alternatives:

(1) I could continue to write about everything except politics and government—become, for example, an expert on foreign policy. The trouble was that I didn't really care enough about foreign policy to become an expert on it, and the topics I did care about—literature and history—were not amenable to daily editorial commentary in newspapers.

(2) I could look for a position writing editorials for a newspaper with whose political views I did agree. But how many of those were there? Mighty, mighty

few American newspapers were of politically liberal allegiance, and of these almost none were in the South, where I wanted to live.

(3) I could leave editorializing and go back to the news side of newspapering, which I respected greatly, and as my friend Guy Friddell had done. Of the three alternatives, this was the most attractive to me. But did I really want to be a reporter again, or for that matter even a columnist?

The answer was no, and moreover, when I considered those alternatives, I knew that I wasn't being honest with myself. They were, if anything, efforts at self-alibi. What I had to confront was the blunt truth that *literature, not journalism, had become my chosen vocation.* In leaving the academic community to return to daily journalism—of any kind, anywhere—*I had made a mistake.* It was literature that I wanted to make my life with—to write about it, teach it, if possible write a little of it myself—and not part-time, not on the side, but as my profession. I might some day be a decent teacher and scholar; but, youthful ambitions notwithstanding, I could never be a really good journalist. *It was not what I wanted to do.*

I realized this now, and therefore I applied myself to getting out of it. To be brief: I wrote letters to various schools, and discovered that my several books, various published essays, and the scholarly acquaintance-

ships I had made while with the American Studies Association had notably enhanced my position in the academic marketplace. I was offered associate professor-
ships of English at the University of Texas and at
Hollins College, near Roanoke, Virginia. I accepted
the Hollins offer, to take effect in the fall of 1957.
Meanwhile I was invited to teach graduate and undergraduate classes in southern history during the
summer term at Louisiana State University in Baton
Rouge, so I was able to give notice to Kilpo to take
effect as of May 1.

By then he already had Jack Hamilton, who was
working on a small newspaper in the Shenandoah Valley, eagerly waiting in the wings. So everyone concerned was happy, myself most of all. To add to the excitement I was awarded a Guggenheim Fellowship,
which I had applied for the previous fall but without
much expectation of getting it. By the end of April
our house had been sold, we packed up everything,
and sixteen months after what I had believed was my
permanent return to Richmond and the profession of
journalism, my wife and I drove off for a month on
Sanibel, in 1957 still a largely undeveloped semitropi-
cal island in the Gulf of Mexico off Fort Myers,
Florida, before reporting at LSU for the summer term.
At Kilpo's request I left the two large portraits of Lee
and Jackson on the outer office wall, swapping them

for a French print of the Seven Days Battles left over
from Dr. Freeman's tenure.

When in September we arrived at Hollins College
for the fall term, counting the three months in Baton
Rouge we had lived in four different cities within little more than three years. Now our wanderings were
done, for another decade at least. The ten years that
followed, 1957–1967, were to be the best years of my
life professionally and personally, for Hollins College
proved to be a superb educational institution and numerous of the students turned into lifelong friends.

Kilpo left Richmond in 1967. By then his syndicated column was being read in newspapers all over
the United States. He was that rare item, a conservative columnist with a first-rate sense of humor, a
throwback to Mencken in what was otherwise mainly
a gallery of long-faced viewers-with-indignation.
When he moved up to Washington his peer group was
no longer the Richmond Establishment but the Washington Press Corps, and it wasn't long before Kilpo
shifted from the far right to a position closer to the
center. In so doing he put racial segregation com-
pletely behind him. He remained a conservative, but
not of the ultra variety. He also began doing network
television commentaries and was soon a household
presence. Always interested in the workings of language, in later years he began producing weekly com-

mentaries on grammar, syntax, vocabulary, and English As It Is Writ in general, which nowadays even those newspaper readers who are far distanced from his politics devour with passion.

So everything worked out for the best for all concerned, and it was to Kilpo that I owed my good fortune. For if I had stayed at the University of Pennsylvania and not come back south to the *News-Leader*, I should very likely have missed going to Hollins, which would have been a deprivation indeed. But that is another story.

\#   \#   \#

8

RESTROSPECTIVE

Someone once asked Flannery O'Connor why she wrote, and her response was, "Because I'm good at it"—which was true, but also something of an evasion, because what she was doing was declining to engage in a public dissection of the complex motives and personal needs that underlay her choice of a vocation. (Anyone wishing to know why Flannery wrote should read her marvelous story "Parker's Back.")

I could offer a similar answer—that I was good at it, too, though not nearly so good as Flannery was—but I am not convinced that aptitude has a great deal to do with the matter, or rather, that aptitude is in itself a sufficient explanation. In my own instance what

I think is that somewhere along the line, very early on, writing became my way of coping with my experience. To write is, after all, an ordering device, a method for defining one's life through re-creating what one perceives and feels in language. In writing something down, one says it is This, or it is That, and not something else. In a quite literal sense, I think on a keyboard—for years a typewriter, more recently a word processor. Until I write something out, I don't know what I think about it.

In a book, for purposes of humor, I once set forth what I termed Rubin's Law: *"All writers are neurotics, but not all neurotics are writers."* That was going a little far, and as a definition it contains several philosophical loopholes. Nonetheless it does seem to me that if one were perfectly adjusted to the world and could live in it without any unease or difficulty whatever, there would be neither need nor desire to write about it. The motivation for writing is to make sense of one's experience, even if no more than to say, "This is what I need to pick up at the supermarket today."

In this book I have been trying to figure out why it was that, while still in my early thirties, I relinquished for good an ambition that since childhood had always been foremost in my thoughts. The preceding series of sketches has been an effort to answer that question for myself. During much of the time I have been describing—roughly, for the first two-thirds of it—the notion I would ever willingly forsake a career as a newspaperman would have been inconceivable.

What I have come to believe is that all along it was not really the newspaper work as such, but the opportunity to write that it offered, that attracted me. Growing up when and where I did, journalism was the form in which a vocation as writer most readily presented itself to me.

As for why I left it, it will not do merely to say that newspaper writing proved to be insufficient for my needs because it did not allow me to go deeply enough and with sufficient complexity into my subject. There are at least two flaws in that argument. For one thing, I can think of not a few very fine journalists, who could never be accused of either superficiality or oversimplification, who made writing for newspapers their life's work, and to the enduring benefit of the audience privileged to read their writings. For another thing, any such proposed explanation cannot answer the question of why it was the field of literary interpretation, not some other area of knowledge, that I chose for my vocation.

I do not think that the choice was an accident. Moreover, I believe that the very element that made literary study so attractive to me would have prevented me from ever becoming a really first-rate newspaperman, and that, without consciously reasoning it out, I had begun to sense just that.

Do not misunderstand. I know that I could write competently enough and to spare, and that I knew a good news story when I saw one, and that although not particularly good at gaining the confidence of public officials I could compensate for that by my energy and range of knowledge. But I lacked a certain mental rigor, a quality of realistic judgment that I cannot quite define, but that enables a good journalist to deal with the news. I think of certain friends of mine who made their lives as working newspapermen. Though very different as individuals, what they had in common was a kind of practicality of approach, one that in no way inhibited the full use of imagination or irony, but that gave authority and directness to all that they wrote.

Whatever this quality or attitude was, I did not possess it, or possess enough of it, to function in whole-souled fashion as a newspaperman, and to be comfortable with doing so. Instead, I preferred to deal with life at one remove, to keep language between myself and direct experience, more or less to approach the world as if it were a metaphor. Quite possibly that preference on my part helped to make me a good teacher and aided me in the kind of sympathetic identification needed to work with writing and writers; I cannot say for sure. But it did not, finally, fit me for the vocation that since childhood I had intended for myself.

More than forty years have gone by since I left my last newspaper job to become a full-time teacher. Since then I have had several careers—as a teacher and scholar, as an occasional jackleg novelist, as an editor of scholarly books and journals, as president and editorial director of a publishing house, and even, in my retirement, as a marine painter. For this I consider myself fortunate; after all, it is not given to all of us to be mediocre in several genres.

Except for the foray into painting, undertaken in my seventies, the common denominator to all these has been writing. Writing is what I do. So long as I am writing I can enjoy various other kinds of activities, related or unrelated to it. When I am not writing, nothing else suffices.

During those years, there has scarcely been a time when I have not been without newspaper ties of some sort. These days I am down to a single once-a-month column for our local paper, which is just enough to allow me to feel that I haven't totally deserted my original allegiance.

What constitutes newspaper work, of course, has changed enormously in the years since I started out

full-time in it shortly after the close of World War II.
The writing process is much the same, and the finished product delivered to the residential doorstep
closely resembles the daily newspaper of a half-century
ago, but from the time that the news is typed out upon
a keyboard to the time when the newspaper comes off
the rotary press, everything is handled differently.

As remarked earlier in this book, in the newspaper
composing rooms of my youth Johannes Gutenberg
and Benjamin Franklin would not have felt techno-
logically bewildered. True, they might at first have
been amazed at the workings of a linotype or an in-
tertype machine, but once they realized that it was no
more than a device for casting rows of letters onto
type-high lead slugs, the rest of the process would not
have differed essentially from what they had done for a
living in Mainz or Philadelphia. By contrast, what
takes place today would utterly baffle them; for one
thing, there would *be* no composing room. Nor would
so much as a single piece of type be in evidence.

I remember the newsroom of the *Charleston Evening
Post* as it was in the late 1930s when I used to write
sports stories for it. It was located on the second floor
of a brick building at 134 Meeting Street in downtown Charleston, across the street from the Gibbes Art
Gallery and next door to the Circular Congregational

Church. In the center of the room, at desks grouped in a semicircle, four reporters—only four; I knew them all—were seated at typewriters, working away. Nearby, behind a long desk, was the city editor, my uncle Manning, in necktie and white shirt with elastic bands to keep his shirtsleeves bunched out of the way, and smoking a Lord Salisbury cigarette of aromatic Turkish tobacco in a long thin holder. At the desk, along with copy spikes, paste pot, copy pencils, wire baskets, a pair of shears, a ruler, and page layout sheets, was a chute for sending copy and receiving proof from the composing room.

Somewhere behind him the telegraph editor, Mr. Losse, was at his desk, and behind was a glass-enclosed room with several rows of teletype machines, steadily rattling out copy. At the opposite end of the room the editor, Mr. Fay Emerson, a family friend who together with my uncle and my father played in the Saturday night poker games in our basement each week, was busy in an adjoining office with editorials, letters to the editor, and editing and headlining the copy of the two women who worked on the society page in another small office next door. On a table just outside his door was a stack of out-of-town newspapers, the exchanges, through which I looked regularly for photos of major league baseball players to clip out and paste in my scrapbook at home.

Across the hall, at a desk that sat out in the hallway just inside the banisters to the stairway, was the associate editor, Mr. Eddie Manigault, who wrote editorials and was the next-in-line in the family who were the principal owners of both the *Evening Post* and the morning paper, the *News and Courier,* the offices of which were back beyond the telegraph cubicle.

At a certain time early each afternoon, from within the recesses of the building somewhere down beneath would come a low rumbling, the floor would commence to vibrate, and minutes later a pressroom worker would emerge from the hallway behind with a stack of first editions, the sheets of newsprint still warm and slightly moist to the touch. That day's issue of the *Charleston Evening Post* was off the press.

There, in that newsroom, was where I wanted someday to be. I never made it.

#   #   #